FRIENDLY VISITING
AMONG THE POOR

PATTERSON SMITH REPRINT SERIES IN
CRIMINOLOGY, LAW ENFORCEMENT, AND SOCIAL PROBLEMS

A listing of publications in the SERIES *will be found at rear of volume*

PUBLICATION NO. 92: PATTERSON SMITH REPRINT SERIES IN
CRIMINOLOGY, LAW ENFORCEMENT, AND SOCIAL PROBLEMS

FRIENDLY VISITING AMONG THE POOR

A Handbook for Charity Workers

BY
MARY E. RICHMOND

With an Introductory Essay
MARY RICHMOND, A FOUNDER
OF MODERN SOCIAL WORK
By MAX SIPORIN

Montclair, New Jersey
PATTERSON SMITH
1969

Originally published 1899
Copyright ©1969 by
Patterson Smith Publishing Corporation
Montclair, New Jersey

SBN 87585-092-8

Library of Congress Catalog Card Number: 69-16244

MARY RICHMOND, A FOUNDER
OF MODERN SOCIAL WORK

MARY RICHMOND, A FOUNDER OF MODERN SOCIAL WORK

"Friendly visiting" as a way of helping the poor is again fashionable. Poor people are again visible; the abolition of poverty is once more a popular public cause. "Maximum feasible participation of the poor" is a battle cry in the current war against inequality and disadvantage, particularly in the ghettos of the big city slums. It is therefore particularly helpful that the classic work on the subject of friendly visiting to the poor should be republished. An historic work of major importance is restored to us. This manual for the training of friendly visitors has a grace of style which maintains its readability and interest. Some aspects of its perspective and procedures belong to a past era. Yet the content has a particular relevance and usefulness in regard to current major needs and issues in the war against poverty in our time.

Mary Ellen Richmond completed writing and saw publication of this handbook in 1899, when she was general secretary of the Charity Organization Society in Baltimore. It is both a pioneer work and a landmark book. It pioneered in its expression of a then new view of poverty. This modern understanding of poverty, which "charity workers" such as Mary Richmond had achieved out of their immediate experiences with the poor, permeates this volume. Because it became a very popular manual, very widely used throughout the country during the next decade, it was one of the influential forces in changing the climate of public opinion to support the epoch-making social legislation and social reforms which were then enacted. Based on this new perspective, *Friendly Visiting Among the Poor* marks an important difference in society's approach to helping the poor, particularly on the part of the charity agencies, and in their use of volunteers. In addition, the book represents a major development of theory and practice for a new professional way of helping people with their social-emotional problems. This helping process came to be called "social work." Mary Richmond was one of the founders of the new profession, and this book was the first of her enduring contributions to its establishment, philosophy and method of practice.

The New View of Poverty

Mary Ellen Richmond was born in Belleville, Illinois, in 1861. She was an only child. Her parents were native to Baltimore, and returned there with her when she was two years of age. Her father, a blacksmith, and her mother both died of tuberculosis when she was a child, and she was reared by relatives. She completed high school, and then did clerical work, for a brief period in New York City, where she lived in abject poverty. Returning to Baltimore, she was bored and frustrated as a bookkeeper and clerk. For many years she looked after a disabled aunt. In 1889, at age 27, Mary Richmond decided to change her employment. By chance she obtained a position as assistant treasurer for the Baltimore Charity Organization Society. She seemed to come to life in this role, learning and doing volunteer visiting on her own initiative and identifying herself completely with her work in providing assistance to the Baltimore poor. Her intellectual brilliance and erudition, her administrative abilities, and her attractive personality (she was described as enthusiastic, self-assured, eloquent and having "magnetic charm") led to her appointment, within less than two years, as head of the agency. She thus joined the mainstream of a social movement against poverty and economic insecurity then gathering momentum, which included the charity organization societies, the social settlements, the religious "social gospel" and labor organizing causes, as well as the radical, populist and progressive political parties.

The charity organization societies and the "friendly

visiting" which distinguished them were ostensibly imported from England during the early 1880s, spreading through the country in response to the economic depression of that decade. However, the actual form of these societies was characteristic of many of the charity and benevolent societies to aid the poor which developed in this country from the early part of the nineteenth century. Thus a structure based on coordinated services in district offices was adopted by the New York Society for the Prevention of Pauperism in 1817, by the Boston Society for the Prevention of Pauperism (founded by Joseph Tuckerman in 1835) and by the New York Association for Improving the Condition of the Poor, or the A.I.C.P., of which Robert M. Hartley became head in 1843. In each of these societies, volunteer visits to the homes of the poor were the central feature of their work. As was later done by the charity organization societies, the New York A.I.C.P. made extensive use of paid district charity workers to train and to complement the work of their volunteers; it also was active in initiating public health, housing and other reforms. However, it was the English pioneers, such as Thomas Chalmers, Octavia Hill and Charles Loch, who provided the inspiring writings and theory for the practice of "charity" and "friendly visiting." Ironically, the practice of "friendly visiting" was largely rejected in England but found ready and wide acceptance in the United States.

The charity organization societies (C.O.S.) presented themselves as practicing "organized" charity work and "scientific philanthropy" in order to help the poor efficiently and economically. This was contrasted with the "indiscriminate almsgiving" and the impersonal outdoor public relief which were condemned as "pauperizing" the poor, in the sense of making people dependent upon public aid. The C.O.S. agencies, which did much to secularize charity, became the predominant form of private volunteer relief assistance to the poor during the late nineteenth century. Their personnel initially regarded poverty in the traditional way, from the viewpoint of the Protestant Ethic, as primarily the result of moral defects and character weaknesses, and as deviant behavior in departing from enshrined norms of self-reliance and self-support. As part of the evolving secular-social institution of social welfare, their major function was both altruistic and repressive. They addressed themselves to giving humanitarian "personal service" in ameliorating widespread destitution and in "rehabilitating" the poor; they served as agents of the well-to-do and middle classes in containing lower-class discontent; they sought to bridge the widening gap between rich and poor and to foster social integration;

and they dealt effectively with the financial and administrative tasks of "charity work" in the urban slums. These functions were based on explicit and carefully rationalized principles of investigation, registration, recording, cooperation and coordination of charitable effort within neighborhoods carried out through the "case work" done by the volunteer committees and visitors in individualizing financial and personal assistance.

The C.O.S. societies codified and systematized procedures for relief and for training of volunteers, but their efficiency resulted in sharp criticism. A contemporary poet wrote that "The organized charity scrimped and iced/In the name of a cautious, statistical Christ." As a representative of the competing social settlements, Jane Addams declared that the settlement "stands not for relief, nor for instruction, but for fellowship."

Nevertheless, it was the charity workers, along with the settlement workers, who accumulated and made available a tremendous amount of social evidence about poverty and who developed new methods of social research and stimulated the great social surveys. Particularly after the severe economic depression of 1893-1894, the charity workers experienced a major change in their perspective about poverty. This is well described by Robert Bremner in his *From the Depths:*

> Beginning as the expression of a somewhat narrow, moralistic and individualistic attitude toward poverty, the charity organization movement ultimately fostered the development of a more broadly social point of view. . . . Knowledge of the misfortunes of hundreds of different families gained through experience as friendly visitors induced many representatives of the organized charities to regard the industrial causes of poverty as more important than the person. . . . Increasingly the agents of organized charity came to look upon the attainment of social justice as a more important field of endeavor than the administration of private benevolence.

The charity workers, in adopting this new view of the causes and nature of poverty, turned increasing attention to adverse social conditions, to economic insecurity, to inadequacies of income and employment and to ill health. They then turned to corrective social legislation as a way of "abolishing" and "preventing" poverty. In rejecting the older connotations of "charity work," they adopted a new name, "social worker," and sought to practice "social work," which terms were in general use by 1905. They became prime movers and leaders of the social reform movement and they fought for and championed innovative social legislation in such fields as housing, child labor, compulsory education, and public health. They became spokesmen and advocates for the poor and crusaders for social justice. Though remaining committed to educational and evolutionary methods of social action and social reform, the social workers were instrumental in forging a new social conscience and an acceptance by society of a new social responsibility, one which began to acknowledge the relief of distress and the provision of a basic standard of living as a right of every citizen.

Mary Richmond expressed this new view of poverty and this new approach to helping the poor in *Friendly Visiting Among the Poor*. There is here a largeness of humanistic spirit and warm sympathy with poor people which is in marked contrast to the moralistic, paternalistic and puritanical exhortations of the older charity organization manuals. Mary Richmond repudiated the older classification of the poor into those "worthy" and "unworthy," and declared that both the poor and the rich could be categorized as workers and parasites. She urged an understanding of the multiple causes of unemployment, rejected the moral and psychological deterministic beliefs about poverty then prevalent, and attributed one fourth of poverty to sickness. While she acknowledged her indebtedness to Jane Addams and the social settlements, she firmly rejected the social determinism of the settlement workers and their belief that poverty is due to social conditions beyond the control of the poor. Rather, she held that the "personal and social causes of poverty act and react upon each other, changing places as cause and as effect, until they form a tangle that no hasty, impatient jerking can unravel."

In consequence, Mary Richmond thought that poverty required both "personal" and "social services," or what she later called the "retail" and "wholesale" forms of social reform. Though her main subject matter in this book is the provision of individualized services, she speaks out for child labor laws and compulsory education for children, attacks the money credit system, and favors the development of recreational facilities for the poor. Along with many of the charity organization leaders, Mary Richmond opposed general public relief and "mothers' pensions," possibly out of a feeling of threat to vested interests, but clearly out of an unrealistic faith in the fulsome generosity of the local communities. Still she expressed a more democratic view than that of her contemporaries, both in her respect for individual differences and in her suggestion that the poor were to be made "partners" by the friendly visitors, so that they could fully participate in the helping process. Here she anticipated the present-day concern for client self-determination and for mutual relations between helper and client.

The Method of Friendly Visiting and Casework

Friendly visiting is a method of helping the poor which goes back to antiquity, being part of the traditional forms of charity within both the Hebrew religious communities and within the medieval Catholic church. In modern times, it became an explicit method of assistance to the poor developed by the secular charity societies. When Charles Loch, the long-term leader of the London Charity Organization Society, described the practice of charity as "love working with discernment," he viewed the function of friendly visiting as expressing the "personal influence" of this "love." Around 1880 Loch began to use the term "case work" to refer to the "case method" of individualization in study of and relief for the poor, as applied by the volunteer committees and visitors. This term had negative connotations for many of the social workers, including Mary Richmond, who opposed the categorization of the "client" as a "case," and resisted giving up the concept and term "friendly visiting." The term "case work" does not appear in this book, and though she later came to employ it as "social case work," she did so only with periodic rebellion, at one point suggesting that it be replaced by the term "social individuation."

Mary Richmond wrote about friendly visiting on

several occasions before and after the publication of this book, always with much esteem and affection. To her, it meant "intimate and continuous knowledge of and sympathy with a poor family's joys, sorrows, opinions, feelings and entire outlook upon life." From an early gushy characterization of friendly visiting as "an uplifting hand, a patient, persevering, faithful friend," she came to speak of it as "intensely personal work." She saw it as "representing the human touch," in offering a corrective for the increasing social class differences of the time, as well as "remedial and preventive measures for dealing with distress in families." A major objective of this work was to develop "the charitable spirit" within the life of the community.

The traditional motto of the friendly visitor, attributed to Octavia Hill, was "Not alms, but a friend." However, the pressure of events forced the visitor to give both alms and friendship, until in time both functions were assumed by the paid and trained charity workers. What is notable about Mary Richmond's approach here is the distinction made between relief giving and friendly visiting, with separate sets of principles set out for each function. This distinction was widely adopted in later years by the voluntary agencies, particularly after the Social Security Act in 1935 explicitly established governmental responsibility for financial relief to those in need, and it is only now in the process of adoption by the public welfare agencies.

It should be noted that Mary Richmond was not too consistent in recognizing in this book that some families could not become self-supporting, yet in viewing relief, (and its denial), as a therapeutic tool in family rehabilitation. This latter idea was not original to her; it was and remains part of the basic doctrine of public welfare assistance. It is only recently that this doctrine has been challenged by the current effort to make a basic minimum income an unconditional right for every member of our society.

Because she was concerned to make friendly visiting more effective, Mary Richmond carefully studied it in order to identify its underlying theory and principles. In *Friendly Visiting Among the Poor,* she stated her early thinking and findings about the helping process, and pulled together the material she developed for training volunteers. It is this thinking which she extended and deepened in her later papers and in her major works, *Social Diagnosis* (1917) and *What is Social Case Work?* (1922).

Mary Richmond's conceptualization of the method of friendly visiting, (which, as noted, she later called "social case work" and which we would now take to include counseling or psychotherapy) is strikingly advanced for its time. She identified its specific objective to be "improving the condition of the family," not only toward self-support, but also toward better family functioning and an improved environment of "healthier surroundings."

The family unit is the focus of diagnosis and treatment here, and this was characteristic of social casework generally up to 1917. Bertha Reynolds (a student of Mary Richmond and a great social work educator) later pointed out that this concern is explained by the fact that the family unit is the basic economic unit of society and therefore it was chosen as the fulcrum for helping people become economically self-supporting. After 1917, the psychiatric ideology captured social work and caseworkers became preoccupied again with the salvation of the individual personality. Mary Richmond herself came to believe that the major objective of social casework is to aid in personal self-realization, and that this is best done "by way of study and better adjustment of man's social relationships."

Mary Richmond gave emphasis to the family unit from a sociological rather than from an economic orientation, and to what we now call the expectations, performances and satisfactions of family roles. She gave particular attention to these aspects in *Friendly Visiting Among the Poor* and in her next book, *The Good Neighbor in the Modern City* (1907), which was about social work and the use of community resources to help people in trouble. She wrote about the father as breadwinner and head of the household; about the wife and mother as homemaker, child-rearer and also as breadwinner; and about the child as family member, with specific needs for growth and development. She attached much importance to the social network in which the family lives, a network of kinfolk, neighbors, friends, employers and church groups, all of which constitute "natural resources" (another important concept she used) for social support and mutual aid. This network, she said, is to be resorted to in preference to "official" agencies. Care is to be taken not to weaken "the ties of neighborliness and mutual dependence among the poor," but to strengthen these through the cooperation and coordination of its elements.

The helping principles given in this book are in some respects similar to those which had already been formulated, by such men as Thomas Chalmers, Baron deGerando, Joseph Tuckerman, Charles Loch and Octavia Hill. Mary Richmond made them more specific and objective. One cardinal principle is that of individualization, which we now refer to as "differential diagnosis and treatment" and which calls for assistance to be given that "will best fit the particular need." Richmond's principles of friendly visiting did nonetheless represent new directions. Her conception of the helping process is more explicitly a problem-solving one, involving study, planning based on "facts," and purposeful action. While the operations remained rather vague, the model of social diagnosis announced in this book has remained the basic model of casework. In *Social Diagnosis* she stated this diagnosis to be "as exact a definition as possible of the social situation and personality of a human being in some social need," thus referring to an inter-related system of problem-person-situation elements. This multi-focal perspective remains a distinguishing characteristic and particular strength of the social work approach to helping people in trouble.

In *Friendly Visiting Among the Poor,* the helping relationship between visitor and the poor person or family is discussed in terms of the use of "personal influence" and of "tact and good will" in a spirit of "trust and friendliness" within a "mutual relationship." Instead of the recent over-emphasis on clinical self-awareness, there is described here an open quality of relationship with the client and a sharing of self (of one's own troubles and experiences) as the basis for constructive helping by the friendly visitor. Thus the visitor is encouraged to "listen patiently," to "strive to see the world from [the homemaker's] point of view," and to believe that "one never feels acquainted with the poor family until [one] has had a good laugh with them." The encouragement of empathy, spontaneity and self-disclosure in the visitor's relationship with clients is very modern in that these are now said to be characteristics of the ideal therapeutic relationship.

The actual work of the visitor is presented here as having primarily an educational and socializing character, as in teaching household and management skills, "educating others in common sense methods," providing enriching learning opportunities, even serving as a role model for the wife, who can "unconsciously imitate" the visitor's (hopefully more positive) attitudes toward the father and children. With the client as partner, the helping process takes place "privately," avoiding "official relations."

There is another important principle which Mary Richmond gave in her paper "The Settlement and Friendly Visiting" (1899) and which she repeated in her later writing on friendly visiting and social casework. This is that all charity work "should render itself unnecessary, . . . extending its activity only in those self-effacing directions which will develop life's natural resources."

We need to take note of certain limitations in this explication of the method of friendly visiting. First, there is a devaluation of racial and ethnic differences in this approach to the poor, who are seen as differing from other members of society primarily on a socio-economic basis. Mary Richmond does relate that her very first visit to a family involved a bed-ridden Negro mother, whom she helped effectively to accept hospitalization, and for the care of whose children she arranged. This story is presented in this book without expressed awareness of racial-ethnic aspects of the case, though she did later accord much more importance to socio-cultural aspects in *Social Diagnosis*. Then, too, sexual aspects of family and marital relationships are avoided by Miss Richmond, who disliked Freud and distrusted the psychoanalytic theories.

More important, there is a serious lack of awareness about psychodynamics and sociodynamics, both about clients and about the helping process. Virginia Robinson was sharply critical of Mary Richmond's "sociological" and "situational approach" when she announced the much greater advantages of Freudian psychoanalytic theory in *A Changing Psychology in Social Casework* (1930). But it is this "situational approach," along with Mary Richmond's enthusiasm for "small group psychology" and for helping families within the context of "normal group settings," that has recently been revived and revitalized, not only for social work, but also for application by the other helping professions. Mary Richmond's definition of social casework as helping essentially "by effecting better adjustments between individuals and their social environment" is now regarded as a crucial element in assistance to individuals and family groups through situational intervention and change. Helping people to improve their social role functioning and relationships is increasingly understood as a direct way of helping them to cope with and resolve their adjustmental and identity problems, including those involving mental illness. And this becomes also a way of aiding people to achieve self-fulfillment and self-actualization.

The Volunteer and the Professional Social Worker

In 1899, when *Friendly Visiting Among the Poor* was published, Mary Richmond for the first time publicly used the terms "social work" and "social worker." She had already committed herself heavily to the advancement of the new profession of social work. In addition to her casework practice and administrative responsibilities, she was increasingly active in social action projects and professional training programs which involved her in national professional affairs. The publication of *Friendly Visiting Among the Poor* gained for her national recognition as a leader in the field of social work.

Also in 1899, Mary Richmond taught for the first

of many times at the Summer School of Applied Philanthropy in New York, which later became the Columbia University School of Social Work. She then decided to leave Baltimore for Philadelphia, where in 1900 she assumed a position as general secretary of the Philadelphia Charity Organization Society. She remained in Philadelphia until 1909, when she moved to New York to become director of the Charity Organization Department of the Russell Sage Foundation. In this latter position she maintained and extended her position as a national leader of the social work profession, doing research, writing, teaching, and helping to establish and expand what are now called "family service agencies" across the country. In 1921, she received an honorary degree from Smith College for "establishing the scientific basis of a new profession." A single woman all her days, she died in New York in 1928.

Along with many of her colleagues, Mary Richmond developed a conception of social work not only as a profession, but also as having a social-institutional function. The economic depression of the mid-1890's led to a rapid increase in the need for and employment of trained, skilled professional social workers. In 1897, Mary Richmond advocated the establishment of a "Training School in Applied Philanthropy," which would provide a two-year course of study. Around that time there was a rapid growth of training programs, particularly within or in conjunction with the new university departments of sociology, and later in separate schools of social work. This development intensified the push toward professionalization on the part of this new breed of social workers.

Following Abraham Flexner's charge in 1915 that social work still was not a profession, there began a process of deliberate specialization and a preoccupation with specialized techniques to justify professional status. Mary Richmond contributed to this trend and to the adoption of a quasi-medical approach in her choice of the concepts of diagnosis and treatment as they applied to social casework, as a way of gaining desirable connotations of skilled scientific objectivity for it. In 1919, in a paper entitled "The Long View," she described the special skill of social casework as helping to adjust individuals and families and social institutions to each other. This helped move social work away from its exclusive concern with the poor. A social-institutional conception of the social work function now regards social services as providing for all of the members of the community, rich and poor.

Even though she was a prime mover in the professionalization of social work, Mary Richmond held fast to her idealistic views about friendly visiting and volunteer work. She believed that the professional social worker could not become "the complete and satisfactory substitute" for the volunteer. The "higher the standard of professional service, the more friendly visitors there will be," was her expressed conviction in 1907. Although friendly visiting merged into casework, it was to the role of the volunteer that she continued to be loyal. The volunteers were to her no longer Lady Bountifuls, but a "non-professional group of social servants . . . the real sons and daughters of the community, while the paid worker, though she may be a loving daughter, is often the adopted one." She held it to be a basic responsibility of trained social workers and social agencies to instruct the volunteer and to guide this work so as to enhance the volunteer's personal growth.

Mary Richmond's pleas for the worth and use of the volunteer were increasingly ignored in the push for professional status, and away from the negative associations of paternalistic charity. There was a long period in which there was a low regard for volunteers, except largely as agency board members and fund raisers. Social workers continued basically to serve and visit in the homes of the poor, as well as to help family groups. But the elite level of social caseworkers in the psychiatric and family agencies withdrew into their offices to practice "therapy" with "sick" individuals, for fees which the voluntary agency system also encouraged.

Happily, these trends have been reversed in recent years, with home visiting and family treatment again in favor, and with a renewed commitment in social work to extensive and comprehensive services to the poor. In this movement, the volunteer and the "indigenous worker" have regained their valued status in social work and in the helping professions generally. Drawn not only from the ranks of the well-to-do and middle-class, but also and especially from the poor, the individual and personal services given by indigenous helpers and volunteers are an essential force in the current war against poverty. These services also are now viewed as the basis for new avocational and vocational careers needed in our service-oriented society. A particular function of these modern-day friendly visitors is to help poor people learn how to cope with the impersonal and complex bureaucracies which have taken over so powerfully in our public and private lives.

Mary Richmond and the Current Scene

Friendly Visiting Among the Poor thus was a pioneer and influential book. In some respects it spoke for a point of view which was then headed for a decline, only to be revived in our time. Toward the end of her life, Mary Richmond described the rhythm of the development of social work as oscillating in a spiral from individual to wholesale methods of social reform, emphasizing individual then social betterment and back again. She recalled that in the decade preceding 1914, the social caseworkers were a discouraged group, "often waved aside as having outlived our usefulness." During that period,

> the great wave of enthusiasm for wholesale measures of reform . . . brought with it many changes which made better social casework possible, but some of the leading social reformers of the period lost their heads to this extent — they were sure that legislation and propaganda, between them, would render social work with and for individuals quite unnecessary, and they did not hesitate to say so.

But then, she said, came "the rediscovery of the individual" and the return to the road of individual betterment. She hoped that the sharp swings of the developmental spiral would end. But unfortunately they have not done so.

It is comforting to recall these remarks during the present social reform era. There has been a return to social determinism, whose adherents are again attacking casework services as inadequate and inefficient in comparison with the promises of social action, social policy changes and social-institutional reform. Although these attacks often represent extremist positions, we may profit from them by recognizing, as Mary Richmond did, that poverty is a multi-factored state of affairs, requiring social policy provisions, as well as individualized services.

The current ideological and power conflicts and the emergence of new needed reforms in services to the poor have evoked a healthy process of upheavals in theory and practice within social work and in the other helping professions. In making the necessary adaptations, we find ourselves resonant with Mary Richmond's situational approach to helping the poor, with her emphasis on friendly home visiting, on family rehabilitation and on educational and socialization methods in the counseling-therapeutic process. We are encouraged to implement her insights into the nurturing and sustaining influences of "friendly relations," of community and "neighboring forces," of social resources and supports in informal as well as formal mutual aid systems.

Friendly Visiting Among the Poor should again prove useful in advancing needed programs of personal friendly services, through trained as well as untrained helpers, to the poor in city slums, as well as to all other people in distress. It should further the utilization of volunteer and indigenous workers who can directly express, mobilize and realize the unofficial systems of aid and support, in acute and chronic crisis situations, with regard to many types of problems. The recent Federal Crime Commission, for example, has strongly urged that, instead of legal and official channels which stigmatize the lawbreaker and juvenile delinquent, much more use should be made of the unofficial rehabilitative relations and community resources to which Mary Richmond attached so much importance. In such ways, then, as Mary Richmond suggested for friendly visiting in this book, we can work "with the democratic spirit of the age to forward the advance of the plain and common people into a better and larger life."

— MAX SIPORIN, D.S.W.

School of Social Work
University of Maryland
July, 1968

PREFACE

THIS little volume is intended as a handbook for those who are beginning to do charitable work in the homes of the poor, whether as individuals or as representatives of some church, or of some religious society, such as the King's Daughters, the Epworth League, or the Christian Endeavor Society. The term "friendly visitor" does not apply to one who aimlessly visits the poor for a little while, without making any effort to improve their condition permanently or to be a real friend to them. Friendly visiting, as distinguished from district visiting, originated with the charity organization societies, some of which are indefatigable in training volunteers to do effective work in the homes of the poor. Though I should be glad to find that my book was of some service to these societies, it was not prepared for their use alone, and no mention is made, therefore, of the organization of visitors into district conferences. For inexperienced workers, who need leadership in their charity, there can be no better training than the meetings of a well-organized conference under a capable chairman, and even the most experienced, by keeping in close touch with such a conference, can do more effective work.

The suggestions herein contained are not to be taken as all applicable to the work of any one visitor. Friendly visitors that tried to adopt them all would have to abandon their other interests, and their other interests make them more useful friends to the poor. Like the words in a dictionary, some suggestions will be of service to a few workers, and others will be found applicable to the work of many.

In addition to the standard authorities mentioned under General References, a list for supplementary reading will be found at the end of each chapter. These lists are in no sense a bibliography of the subject. A handbook such as this is chiefly useful in suggesting further inquiry, and, for beginners, I have thought best to include a number of references out of the beaten track to stories and magazine articles that seemed illustrative of the matter in hand.

It will be seen that I have borrowed much in direct quotation in the following pages from those who have preceded me in writing about the poor, but my debt does not end here. Whatever I may be said to know about charitable work — my whole point of view and inspiration in fact — can be traced to certain definite sources. To some of the leaders of the Charity Organization Society of London, to Miss Octavia Hill, Mrs. Bernard Bosanquet, and Mr. C. S. Loch, it will be evident to my readers that my obligation is great. It will be evident also that I have been helped by Mrs. Josephine Shaw Lowell and other workers in New York, who, against such odds, are making advances in the reform of municipal abuses; and by that group too who, under the leadership of Miss Jane Addams, have given us, at Hull House in Chicago, so admirable an object lesson in the power of neighborliness. But more than to any other teachers, perhaps, I am indebted to those members of the Associated Charities who organized Boston's friendly visitors nineteen years ago, and have led them since to increasing usefulness. Their reports have been my most valuable source of information. If I do not name also my friends and fellow-workers here in Baltimore, it is not because I fail to bear them individually most gratefully in mind.

BALTIMORE, January, 1899.

CONTENTS

Mary Richmond,
 a Founder of Modern Social Work . . . v

Preface xxxi

CHAPTER I
Introduction 1

CHAPTER II
The Breadwinner 17

CHAPTER III
The Breadwinner at Home 44

CHAPTER IV
The Homemaker 64

CHAPTER V
The Children 76

CHAPTER VI
Health 95

CHAPTER VII
Spending and Saving 108

CHAPTER VIII
Recreation 127

CHAPTER IX
Relief 140

CHAPTER X
The Church 166

CHAPTER XI
The Friendly Visitor 179

APPENDIX 197

INDEX 219

GENERAL REFERENCES

Proceedings of National Conferences of Charities and Correction, 25 volumes, especially portions containing reports of sections on Child-Saving and Organization of Charities. The Conference Reports constitute the best American authority on charities. Special papers in the Reports are noted in this book after the appropriate chapters.

Proceedings of International Congress of Charities, Correction and Philanthropy, Chicago, 1893, especially volumes on "Care of Children" and "Organization of Charities." Published by Johns Hopkins Press, Baltimore.

"Homes of the London Poor," Octavia Hill. For sale by New York State Charities Aid Association, 25 cents.

"Essays," Octavia Hill. For sale by Boston Associated Charities; price, 10 cents.

"Rich and Poor," Mrs. Bernard Bosanquet.

"How to help the Poor," Mrs. James T. Fields.

"Public Relief and Private Charity," Mrs. Josephine Shaw Lowell.

"American Charities," A. G. Warner.

"Hull House Maps and Papers."

FRIENDLY VISITING AMONG THE POOR

CHAPTER I

INTRODUCTION

THERE is a certain development in the English novel of which I have long seemed to be vaguely conscious. At one time I hoped to set myself the task of tracing it, though I have since relinquished all thought of this as too ambitious. The movement — if, indeed, there be such a movement — has always pictured itself to my mind as the march of the plain and common people into the foreground of English fiction. I venture to introduce the idea here, though it may appear foreign to my subject, as illustrating another and equally important movement in the development of charitable work.

Should any one ever turn over the pages of our two centuries' stock of novels, with a view to tracing this gradual development of interest in the poor and unfortunate, he would find, of course, that facts have a tantalizing way of moving in zigzags whenever one is anxious that they should move forward in a straight line; but he would probably find also that, in the earlier attempts of the novel writer to picture the poor, they were drawn as mere puppets on which the richly endowed heroes and heroines exercised their benevolence. Very likely he would discover that, when at last the poor began to take an important part in the action of the story, we were permitted to see them at first only through a haze of sentimentality, so that, allowing for great advances in the art of novel writing between the time of Richardson and the time of Dickens, we still should find the astonishing characterizations of " Pamela " reflected in the impossible virtues and melodramatic vices of Dickens' poor people.

To Miss Edgeworth and Scott first, perhaps, and to George Eliot most of all, we should find ourselves indebted for faithful studies of plain people, — studies made with an eye single to the object, and leaving, therefore, no unlovely trait slurred over or excused, yet giving us that perfect understanding of every-day people which is the only true basis of sympathy with them. In America we are indebted to such conscientious artists as Miss Jewett and Octave Thanet for a similar enlargement of our sympathies through their life-like pictures of the less sophisticated people of our own time.

An even more recent development would be found in what is called the "sociological" novel. Monstrous and misshapen as this must seem to us often, if considered as a work of art, it would have to be reckoned with in any investigation of the treatment of poverty in fiction.

Turning to the treatment of poverty in fact, it is surely not altogether fanciful to think that we can trace a similar development, — the march of the plain and common people into the foreground of the charitable consciousness. Here, too, the facts will not always travel in straight lines, and the great souls of earlier ages will be found to have anticipated our best thinking; but usually the world has failed in any effort to adopt their high standards. Speaking roughly, several centuries of charitable practice, in the English world at least, are fairly well summed up in the doggerel verses of that sixteenth-century divine, quoted by Hobson, who counselled his flock,

> "Yet cease not to give
> Without any regard;
> Though the beggars be wicked,
> Thou shalt have *thy* reward."

The spirit of the mediæval church, too, encouraged charitable giving in the main "as a species of fire insurance." The poor, when they were thought of at all, were too likely to be regarded as a means of saving the giver's soul. This view of poverty is either quite dead or dying, but the sentimental view, which succeeded it, is still very common. We are still inclined to take a conventional attitude toward the poor, seeing them through the comfortable haze of our own excellent intentions, and content to know that we wish them well, without being at any great pains to know them as they really are. In other words, our intentions are good, but they are not always good enough to lead us to take our charitable work quite seriously, and found it solidly upon knowledge and experience.

But the century drawing to a close has seen two very important developments in charitable work in England and America; developments quite as important in their own field as the advances of the century in the art of fiction. The first of these is the wonderful growth of the spirit of individual service, which has found one of its highest expressions in the work of friendly visitors in the homes of the poor. The second is the new but vigorous growth of the spirit of social service, which has found its best expression in social and college settlements. It might be possible to prove that both these developments are merely revivals, that at several stages of the world's history the same ideas have been put forward under other names; but never before, as it seems to me, have they found such general recognition.

This gives us three tolerably well-defined phases of charitable progress: the phases of indiscriminate relief, of individual service, and of social service. In the first phase, we are charitable either for the sake of our souls or else to gratify our own emotions. In the second, we are charitable for the sake of the individual poor man. In the third, we are charitable for the sake of the class to which he belongs.

Of the dangers of indiscriminate relief, it should not be necessary to speak, for much has been written on that subject; but the dangers of individual and social service have not been so frequently pointed out. These two forms of service are very closely related. It is impossible to treat the individual poor man without affecting the condition of his fellows for better or worse, and it is impossible to deal with social conditions without affecting the units that compose society. The problems of poverty must be attacked from both sides, therefore, and though I shall dwell particularly upon individual service in these pages, we should remember that, unless this service is supplemented by the work of good citizens, who shall strive to make our cities healthier and freer from temptation, our school system more thorough and practical, and our public charities more effective, unless this public work also is pushed forward, our individual work in the homes of the poor will be largely in vain.

I have said that there were dangers in both forms of service. In work with individual poor families we are likely to forget that these are part of a neighborhood and community, and that we have no right to help them in a way that will work harm to the community. We are always inclined to think that the particular family in which we are interested is an "exceptional case," and the exceptional treatment lavished upon our exceptional case often rouses in a neighborhood hopes that it is impossible for us to fulfil. Then, too, occupied as we are with individuals, we are likely to exaggerate the importance of those causes of poverty that have their origin in the individual. We are likely to over emphasize the moral and mental lacks shown in bad personal habits, such as drunkenness and licentiousness, in thriftlessness, laziness, or inefficiency; and some of us are even rash enough to attribute all the ills of the poor to drink or laziness. On the other hand, those who are engaged in social service often exaggerate the causes of poverty that are external to the individual. Bad industrial conditions and defective legislation seem to them the causes of nearly all the distress around them. Settlement workers are likely to say that the sufferings of the poor are due to conditions over which the poor have no control.

The truth lies somewhere between these two extremes; the fact being that the personal and social causes of poverty act and react upon each other, changing places as cause and as effect, until they form a tangle that no hasty, impatient jerking can unravel. The charity worker and the settlement worker have need of each other: neither one can afford to ignore the experience of the other. Friendly visitors and all who are trying to improve conditions in poor homes should welcome the experience of those who are studying trade conditions and other more general aspects of questions affecting the welfare of the poor. But they should not permit themselves to be swept away by enthusiastic advocates of social reform from that safe middle ground which recognizes that character is at the very centre of this complicated problem; character in the rich, who owe the poor justice as well as mercy, and character in the poor, who are masters of their fate to a greater degree than they will recognize or than we will recognize for them. To ignore the importance of character and of the discipline that makes character is a common fault of modern philanthropy. Rich and poor alike are pictured as the victims of circumstances, of a wrong social order. A political writer has said that formerly, when our forefathers became dissatisfied, they pushed farther into the wilderness, but that now, if anything goes wrong, we run howling to Washington, asking special legislation for our troubles. Symptoms are not lacking of a healthy reaction from this undemocratic attitude of mind. In so far as our charitable work affects it, let us see to it that we do our part in restoring a tone of sturdy self-reliance and independence to the Commonwealth.

Turning from these more general considerations, it is proposed, in this book, to treat of various aspects of the home life of the poor as affected by charity. At the very beginning, however, it may be well to inquire, Who are the poor? If this were a study of the needs of the rich, we should realize at once that they are a difficult class to generalize about; rich people are understood to differ widely from each other in tastes, aims, virtues, and vices. The great, conglomerate class of the rich — which is really no social class at all — has included human beings as different as Lord Shaftesbury and Mr. Barney Barnato. But it is the very same with the poor; and any effort to go among them for the purpose of helping them that does not frankly recognize this wide diversity, must end in failure. The charity worker must rid himself, first of all, of the conventional picture of the poor as always either very abjectly needy, or else very abjectly grateful. He must understand that an attitude of patronage toward the poor man is likely to put the patron in as ridiculous a position as Mr. Pullet, when he addressed his nephew, Tom Tulliver, as "Young Sir." Upon which George Eliot remarks: "A boy's sheepishness is by no means a sign of overmastering reverence; and while you are making encouraging advances to him under the idea that he is overwhelmed by a sense of your age and wisdom, ten to one he is thinking you extremely queer." The would-be philanthropist, who is very conscious of himself and only vaguely conscious of the object of his benevolence, is likely to seem and to be "extremely queer."

If I were writing about the rich, I should be inclined to divide them, according to their attitude toward life, into workers and parasites, but this classification will serve for the poor as well. The motto of the worker is, "I owe the world a life," and the motto of the parasite is, "The world owes me a living." When the parasite happens to be poor we call him a pauper; but there is a world of difference between poverty and pauperism. The poor man may become destitute through stress of circumstances, and be forced to accept charity, but your true pauper, be he rich or poor, has the parasitic habit of mind. When we ask ourselves then, Who are the poor? we must answer that they include widely divergent types of character, — the selfish and the unselfish, the noble and the mean, workers and parasites — and that, in going among them, we must be prepared to meet human beings differing often from ourselves, it may be, in trivial and external things, but like ourselves in all else.

Some who are ready enough to recognize these rudimentary facts about the poor, question our right to go among them with the object of doing them good, regarding it as an impertinent interference with the rights of the individual. But those who hold to this view seldom have the courage of their convictions. When they see suffering, they are very likely to interfere by sending help, though this well-meant interference, unaccompanied by personal knowledge of all the circumstances, often does more harm than good, and becomes a temptation rather than a help. We must interfere when confronted by human suffering and need. Why not interfere effectively? Why not do our best to remove the causes of need?

Many earnest workers in charity feel that social conditions could be wonderfully improved if, to every family in distress, could be sent a volunteer visitor, who would seek out and, with patience and sympathy, strive to remove the causes of need. Such a visitor must have the courage and self-control to confine his work to a few families, for it is impossible to know many well, to understand all their temptations and difficulties, and so help them effectively. To supply every needy family with a friend may seem an impossible ideal, but if all who are undoing each other's work to-day by doing it twice over, and if all who now waste their time in unnecessary charities, were seriously to put themselves in training, and confine their work to the thorough treatment of a few families, the problem of how to help the poor would be solved.

The introduction to such work might come in many ways. It might come through our natural relations as employers or neighbors or church members, or it might come through the district office of a charity organization society, for these societies usually make a specialty of training volunteers and of establishing friendly relations between volunteer visitors and needy families. But come as it may, an introduction can be made for us, and we need not enter the poor man's home as an intruder.

Much has been written about the qualifications necessary for charitable work. It is possible to exaggerate them. Those who are unfamiliar with the homes of the poor are likely to think it unsafe to send young and inexperienced people into poor neighborhoods. As a matter of fact, there are many good people in the poorest neighborhoods, and young workers are as safe there as anywhere. In an old note-book I find that years ago I set down the necessary qualifications of the friendly visitor to be tact and good-will. If we consider that tact includes knowledge, either instinctive or acquired, this may still stand. We cannot be tactful with those whose point of view we fail to understand, or do not even strive to understand. The best helps toward such an understanding, and the best training for charitable work, must come from life itself. If we take no interest in the joys and sorrows of human beings, if we show neither judgment nor energy in the conduct of our own affairs, if life seem to us, on the whole, a flat and unprofitable affair, then no amount of reading will transform us into good friendly visitors. Given the tactful, kindly spirit, with a dash of energy added, study and experience can teach us how to turn these to the best account in the service of others. Our reading must be supplementary to experience, of course, and can in no wise take the place of it.

Leaving all further generalization about friendly visiting for the last chapter, in the following pages my point of departure will be the organization of the poor man's home rather than the organization of charity. The head of the family as citizen, employee, husband, and father; the wife as homemaker; the children; the family health and recreations; the principles involved in spending and saving; the principles of effectual relief; the relations of the church to the poor, — these will be considered in turn. Necessarily, in a book of this size, the attempt must be to suggest lines of inquiry and points of view, rather than to treat adequately any one part of the subject.

Collateral Readings: "Individuality in the Work of Charity," George B. Buzelle in Proceedings of Thirteenth National Conference of Charities, pp. 185 *sq*. "Scientific Charity," Mrs. Glendower Evans in Proceedings of Sixteenth National Conference of Charities, pp. 24 *sq*. Chapters on "Scientific Charity" in "Problems of American Society," J. H. Crooker. Papers on Social Settlements in Proceedings of Twenty-third National Conference of Charities, pp. 106 *sq*. "The Causes of Poverty," F. A. Walker in "Century," Vol. LV, pp. 210 *sq*. "The Jukes," Richard Dugdale. "Tribe of Ishmael," Oscar McCulloch in Proceedings of Fifteenth National Conference of Charities, pp. 154 *sq*. "The Rooney Family," see Charles Booth's "Life and Labor of the People," Vol. VIII, pp. 317 *sq*. "Life in New York Tenement Houses," William T. Elsing in "Scribner's," Vol. XI, pp. 677 *sq*. "An Experiment in Altruism," Miss Margaret Sherwood.

CHAPTER II

THE BREADWINNER

A CONFERENCE was held in one of our large cities lately of half a dozen church and charity workers, who had been called together to make some plan or agree upon some common principle in dealing with a certain family, to whom charitable relief had been given in an aimless way for many years with no good result. Three churches were represented, and the persons present had visited and relieved the family for periods ranging from three to ten years. Almost immediately, however, the fact was brought out at the conference that not one of these visitors had ever seen the man of the family, or had ever made any effort to see him. By way of excuse one visitor said she had always understood that the man was very good-for-nothing. But happily there is no better dispeller of mental fog than a friendly conference of those who are in earnest, and it did not take long to convince these conferees that the man's good-for-nothingness was, in part at least, their own fault. I shall have occasion to speak more than once, in this book, of the power of suggestion. Even here, where these relief visitors had never given the head of the family a thought, they had taught him a lesson. From their whole line of conduct he must have received the suggestion that his neglect of his family was an affair of no consequence.

In turning to the details of family life among the poor, I take the breadwinner, or the one who ought to be the breadwinner, as my first consideration for the reason that he is so often ignored altogether by charity workers. Especially is this true of church workers. "A church worker came to me the other day," writes Mrs. Bosanquet, "about a family of little children, concerning whom he was greatly distressed. He had visited them for months, and found the woman honest, striving, and clean, but *as usually happens* he knew very little of the man. He assured me over and over again that the family was in a pitiable state of poverty and in urgent need of help; and we at once set to work to ascertain the real financial position. Result: man earning 35*s*., giving 20*s*. to his wife and keeping 15*s*. for pocket-money. Obviously, if charity steps in here, it will not necessarily improve the state of the wife and children at all; it will merely enable the man to keep a still larger proportion of his wages for pocket-money." [1]

But, though the charity worker may ignore the man of the family, there are others who are wiser. In the first place he is a voter, and the ward-worker, the policeman, and the saloon-keeper never forget this fact.

An illustration of the policeman's interest in the voter as an applicant for charity may be found wherever the police are allowed to become distributors of alms. In Baltimore the police have been allowed to distribute relief intrusted to them by private citizens, and have been in the habit of making public appeals for such contributions to aid the poor

[1] "Rich and Poor," p. 211.

in cold weather. One policeman, who had a difficult beat, where there were many toughs and criminals, said that the distribution of police relief made his work easier, as toughs whose families had been relieved did not trouble him so much. It is an interesting fact that, during the hard times of 1893-94, political clubs vied with each other the country over in distributing aid. Leaders of Tammany Hall were shrewd enough to urge their followers to organize relief distributions in every district of New York.

It is well to realize that much of the political corruption of our large cities may be traced to the simple fact that the poor man is like ourselves: he follows the leaders personally known to him, and to whom he is personally known. He is sometimes a venal voter, but more often he is only an ignorant voter, who, while innocently following the man that has taken the trouble to do him a favor or to be socially agreeable to him, is handicapping himself and his children with dirty streets, an unsanitary home, an overcrowded school, an insufficient water supply, blackmailing officials, and all those other abuses of city government which press with peculiar hardship upon the poor. The question of municipal reform is inextricably connected with any effort to improve the condition of the poor in their homes, and no charity worker can afford to ignore this connection.

In "Problems of Modern Democracy," Mr. E. L. Godkin says: "Nothing is more surprising in the attempt to deal with the problems of urban life than the way in which religious and philanthropic people ignore the close connection between municipal politics and the various evils about which they are most concerned. All the churches occupy themselves, in a greater or less degree, with the moral condition of the poor. Charitable associations spend hundreds of thousands every year in trying to improve their physical condition. A conference of Protestant ministers met in this city two years ago to consider the best means of reviving religious interest among the working classes and inducing a larger number of them to attend church on Sundays. Of course these gentlemen did not seek an increase in the number of churchgoers as an end in itself. The Protestant churches do not, as the Catholic church does, ascribe any serious spiritual efficacy to mere bodily presence at religious worship. Protestant ministers ask people to go to church in the hope that the words which they will hear with their outward ears may be so grafted inwardly in their hearts that they may bring forth the fruit of good living. What was remarkable in the debates of this conference, therefore, was the absence of any mention of the very successful rivalry with religion which, as an influence on the poor and ignorant foreign population, politics in this city carries on. The same thing may be said, *mutatis mutandis*, of the charitable associations. No one would get from their speeches or reports an inkling of the solemn fact that the newly arrived immigrant who settles in New York gets tenfold more of his notions of American right and wrong from city politics than he gets from the city missionaries, or the schools, or the mission chapels; and yet such is the case. I believe it is quite within the truth to say that, as a moral influence on the poor and ignorant, the clergyman and philanthropist are hopelessly distanced by the politician."[1]

It has been said that, in the effort to establish friendly relations with a poor man, often the greatest lack is a common topic. Here is at least one topic that rich and poor have in common. Here it will be found too that they have many grievances in common, and what makes a better beginning for a friendly relation than a common grievance? Another common topic, and a related one, is the news of the day. More often than not, even the very poor read the daily papers.

Beside the ward politician, the saloon-keeper, and the policeman, there are others who take an interest in the breadwinner. If he is injured, or his property is injured, there are third-rate lawyers ready to bring suit for half the proceeds — an unduly expensive arrangement for the man that has a good claim. If he would save, there are agents of unsound financial schemes ready to take advantage of his ignorance. If he would borrow, there are

[1] pp. 141 *sq.*

chattel-mortgage sharks ready to burden him with a debt at ruinous interest. If he would buy, there are instalment dealers ready to tempt him into buying more than he can afford, and ready to charge two prices for their wares. Whole industries are created to take advantage of his lack of shrewdness, and every effort of his to get on, to get out of the old groove, is resisted by such agencies. Surely, if any one stands in need of a friend, who will patiently strive to see the world through his eyes, and yet will have the courage to tell him the plain truth, it is the breadwinner.

But that picture would be a distorted one which represented the poor man as friendless save for the politicians. His neighbors and companions are in no position to protect him from the foes I have mentioned, but their neighborliness is none the less genuine. Most patient and long-suffering of neighbors are the small landlords who sublet. The tradesmen in poor neighborhoods are also heavy losers. When a family applies for the first time to a church or charity, it often means that they have been aided most generously for a long time by neighbors and small dealers. Sometimes one happens upon the very best and most thoughtful charity given in this way. A Boston worker tells of a street-car conductor, not only supported through the winter by his fellow-conductors, but faithfully nursed by them at night, each one taking turns after the long day's work. Such glimpses as this show us how queer is our usual charitable perspective, in which, as in a picture on a Chinese fan, we see the church steeple in the middle distance and the church visitor looming large in the foreground, while the poor little object of charity, quite helpless and alone save for us, huddles in a corner. The fact is that every life has a background, if we will but take the trouble to see and understand it: all the barrenness is in our own imaginations.

When the poor man attempts to be charitable without knowledge, he is just as clumsy as the rest of us. Writing of "The Attitude of Workingmen toward Modern Charity," Miss Clare de Graffenreid says: "A notable instance of reckless giving came under my observation just after the great strike in the mining regions, when a man who had lost both arms went begging in Georges Creek Valley. How he was maimed, whether he was worthy, proved immaterial. Nor does it appear that he was even a miner; but he asked alms at all the mines. Now the miners had had no money since they were paid off for April, the strike having begun on the 7th of May and having lasted until the 1st of July, while some workers were unable to secure employment until later. After two months and more of idleness the men had either used their savings to live on or were deeply in debt, or both. They could hope for no money until their July labor was paid for in August. In the latter part of July came this armless stranger, who personally solicited these big-hearted coal diggers, and received, without investigation on their part, written subscriptions for various amounts, to be withheld next pay-day from their wages. From the mines of one company alone the man presented to the paymaster orders amounting to three hundred dollars; and the superintendent believes that this one beggar during a short stay in the Valley obtained fully a thousand dollars, if not more. Nor did the enterprising mendicant trouble himself to remain to collect these sums in person. He gave a Chicago address to which checks for the total amounts subscribed in each mine were sent; and he went away to 'work' some other field." [1]

These facts stand side by side. The poor man is often able to do the very best charitable work, acting with a full knowledge of the circumstances, with quick sympathy, and entire unselfishness. On the other hand, when considerations of public welfare, or conditions outside his personal experience complicate the situation, his charity is sometimes reckless and harmful.

Another fact to bear in mind is that the ties of neighborliness and mutual dependence among the poor can be weakened by a charity that leaves such natural and healthful relations out of account. The poor in rich neighborhoods, or in neighborhoods where alms are lavishly given, are less kind to each other, and the whole tone of a neighborhood can be lowered,

[1] "Charities Record," Baltimore, Vol. I, No. 6.

mistrust and jealousy being substituted for neighborly helpfulness, by undiscriminating doles from those whose kindly but condescending attitude has quite blinded them to the everyday facts of the neighborhood life. There are some who think it a pity that, out of their slender store, the poor should give to the still poorer; they feel that the rich should relieve the poor of this burden. But relief given without reference to friends and neighbors is accompanied by moral loss; poor neighborhoods are doomed to grow poorer and more sordid, whenever the natural ties of neighborliness are weakened by our well-meant but unintelligent interference.

Turning to the breadwinner as an employee, we are confronted with the gravest questions now occupying public attention: with the organization of labor, the strike, the lockout, the rights of capital, the problem of the unemployed, and of the unskilled laborer. The truth about these matters, even if one were so fortunate as to possess the truth about them, is not to be stated in a paragraph or a chapter.

Only in so far as they directly concern the friendly visitor to the families of the least fortunate class of workers, can questions of employment be even mentioned in these pages. The more the visitor studies and thinks of them, however, the better friend he can be to the poor. Partly because they are difficult, and partly because our prejudices are involved, the charitable are too prone to dodge economic issues.

We should ask ourselves fearlessly the object of all our charitable work. As Mrs. Bosanquet says: "We need to be quite sure that we really *want* to cure poverty, to do away with it root and branch. Unless we are working with a whole-hearted and genuine desire toward this end, we shall get little satisfaction from our efforts; but those who share unreservedly in this desire are comparatively few at present. Only the other day I heard it said that it was a very doubtful policy to aim at curing poverty, for that in the absence of poverty the rich would have no one upon whom to exercise their faculty of benevolence; and I believe that this was but an outspoken expression of a feeling which is still very prevalent, the feeling that there is something preordained and right in the social dependence of one class upon another. There is the lurking fear, also, that if the working classes get too independent the rich man may suffer for it. 'It won't do,' said one wise lady, 'to make them too independent; they go and join trade-unions, and a friend of mine lost quite a lot of money because his workmen joined a trade-union.' This is quite in the vein of the old Quarterly Reviewer, who summed up the current objections to the Owenite schemes of coöperation as 'the fear that the working classes might become so independent that the unworking classes would not have sufficient control over them, and would be ultimately obliged to work for themselves.'" [1]

The ability of the friendly visitor to put behind him his own personal prejudices and selfish interests, and look at all questions of employment with reference to the best interests of the workers, is of the first importance. Such questions are often very complicated.

[1] "Rich and Poor," pp. 138 *sq.*

An inquiry was sent out in 1896 to the charity organization societies of the country, asking whether these societies approved of supplying workers to take the place of striking employees. The answers, as reported in the proceedings of the Twenty-third National Conference of Charities,[1] seem to take it for granted that either all strikes are equally justifiable or else equally unjustifiable; the fact being, of course, that some strikes are entirely justifiable, that others are quite the reverse, and that still others, which are justifiable at one stage, become unjustifiable at another stage, where the ground of contention has been shifted.

It is about such complicated relations as these that we must inform ourselves when we dare to interfere, and charitable societies cannot afford to adopt any patent formula with regard to them; they must be courageous enough and intelligent enough to bear their part in the solution of industrial questions. The individual friendly visitor may be called upon at any time to advise an unemployed

[1] pp. 242 *sq.*

workman whose only immediate chance of work is in replacing a striker. His family may be destitute, and their troubles may press heavily upon the visitor, who sees in the offered work an easy solution of their difficulties. But the visitor's duty toward the family does not end with their material needs, and, unless the man who replaces the striker is sure that the strike deserves to fail, he will have done an unmanly thing in betraying his natural allies. All question of the right of individual contract aside, he will have injured himself, he will be a meaner man and a less worthy head of a family. Charity cannot afford to ignore this possible result for any temporary and material advantage. Nor will it be enough for the friendly visitor to believe that the particular strike is an unjustifiable one; the man himself must believe it.

Other things being equal, a man is stronger and steadier for having a trade that is well organized, one that has its trade code of ethics. It is safe to say, therefore, that a visitor is justified in advising non-union men to join trade-unions, and that he is not committing himself to an endorsement of every act of every trade-union in so doing.

But applicants for charity are not usually skilled workmen, and most of the work of the friendly visitor will be with those whose occupations are still unorganized, with porters, day-laborers, stevedores, etc. In spite of many assertions to the contrary, it would seem that, in ordinary times, there is still work somewhere for those who have the will and the skill to do it. The charity worker has discouragements enough without allowing himself to be demoralized by the wild talk about millions of skilled workers out of work. During times of panic, even, the number of the unemployed is often grossly exaggerated.[1]

The fact which most directly concerns us is that a large majority of those who are thrown upon charity through lack of employment are either incapable or are unfit for service through bad habits, bad temper, lack of references, ignorance of English, or through some physical defect. Experience has proven that a certain proportion of these can be re-

[1] See Warner's "American Charities," pp. 177 *sq.*

instated in the labor market if we are careful (1) not to make it too easy for them to live without work, (2) if we will use every personal endeavor to fit them for some kind of work, and (3) help them to find and keep the work for which they are fitted. "Character is not cut in marble; it is not something solid and unalterable. It is something living and changing, and may become diseased as our bodies do."[1] Like our bodies, too, it may be made whole again by skilful treatment.

Those who are simply incapable, without bad habits or other defects, are often the victims of their parents' necessities or greed: they were put to work too early, and at work where there was no chance of education or promotion. Sometimes they have been wilfully careless and lazy, but, more often, the fault was either with the parents or with an economic condition that denied them proper training. Of all this we shall hear in connection with the children, but our present concern is with the breadwinner. The man who "does not know how" is the football of in-

[1] George Eliot in "Daniel Deronda."

dustry; employed in work requiring nothing but muscle, promptly discharged because easily replaced, he drifts from job to job, and, at certain seasons of the year, being unable to adapt himself or easily change from one kind of work to another, he is almost certain to be unemployed.

Miss Octavia Hill calls attention to this in "Homes of the London Poor."[1] "The fluctuations of work cause to respectable tenants the main difficulties in paying their rent. I have tried to help them in two ways. First, by inducing them to save; this they have done steadily, and each autumn has found them with a small fund accumulated, which has enabled them to meet the difficulties of the time when families are out of town. In the second place, I have done what I could to employ my tenants in slack seasons. I carefully set aside any work they can do for times of scarcity, and I try so to equalize in this small circle the irregularity of work, which must be more or less pernicious, and which the childishness of the poor makes doubly so. They have

[1] pp. 22 *sq*.

strangely little power of looking forward; a result is to them as nothing if it will not be perceptible until next quarter!"

This plan of equalizing work by saving our odd jobs for dull seasons is one way of helping. Another is to seek lists of unskilled and seasonal occupations that do not overlap. Some work is naturally winter work, and some naturally belongs to the summer season. The ice companies in Baltimore employ their workers in winter by combining the coal business with the ice business, and, on this principle, a list could be drawn up for each community of occupations that do not overlap. No list can be given here, because the conditions of work vary in different parts of the country.

When we furnish work ourselves we must be careful not to confound the employer with the friend. "A visitor was interested in a woman who needed work very much, and herself employed her," writes the secretary of the Boston Associated Charities, Miss Z. D. Smith. "Once or twice it happened that the woman had to go to court in the morning, and came at ten instead of eight, or again the visitor let her off early, but she always paid her for the whole day. The visitor was advised that in the long run it was unwise not to pay her by the hour, as was the custom, but she was not convinced until, having got work for her among her neighbors, they complained that she came at ten instead of eight, and expected pay for the whole day, and they would not employ her longer. The relief the visitor gave, disguised as pay, defeated her efforts to help the woman to self-support."[1]

Bad habits as a cause of unemployment will be considered in the next chapter. As to the man who loses his work through bad temper, it is well to bear in mind that there are many degrees of badness of temper, and the bad temper that comes from worry or ill health must be carefully distinguished from innate ugliness. Lack of references, another cause of unemployment, does not always mean a bad record. Unskilled workers are often personally unknown to their employers, and the knowledge that a visitor can acquire by testing a worker may become a great help to him. When a

[1] "Charities Review," Vol. II, p. 54.

man has some physical defect, such as an impediment in his speech, or a crippled arm, only one who takes a personal interest in him can overcome the prejudice created by his defect. Often such people have qualities that would recommend them, but they are awkward in pleading their own cause or in finding their right niche.

The following illustrations of timely help in finding employment are taken from the Twenty-eighth Report of the Charity Organization Society of London.[1] "One was a quiet, honest young fellow, a gardener, who had lately come out of a lunatic asylum, his insanity being due, it appeared, to ear trouble, involving a painful operation. He had been some months in the asylum, and on coming out was at some loss to obtain regular employment. The Committee, having thoroughly investigated the case and satisfied themselves of the safety of recommending the young man, issued a circular to gardeners and nurserymen, which got him a job within a week. The other man had been noticed in the infirmary — a big, strong fellow,

[1] p. 11.

most of his life a seaman, and part of it on board an American man-of-war, till he met with an accident resulting in the loss of one of his legs. Then he had to come ashore, and a restless, roving disposition led him to tramp about the country, and brought him on one occasion before a London police magistrate for attempting to commit suicide. Inquiry showed that the man could work hard, and, strange to say of a man over six feet high and broad in proportion, was handy with his needle at embroidery, etc. The Committee kept him a few nights at a common lodging-house — for he was homeless since leaving the infirmary — and then by great good fortune got him work at a tent and sail maker's, where now, some half a year later, he is earning his 3*s.* 6*d.* a day. It is to be noted that neither of these men was able-bodied. The Society *does not* try to find work for ordinary, able-bodied men."

Ignorance of English has been given as another cause of lack of employment, but this is not irremovable. "After many days' searching, work was found for Mr. H. and his son, whose ignorance of our language was so entire that they failed to get employment, and were in despair. At the earnest request of the visitor, a furniture dealer consented to take them on trial; and they proved so satisfactory that they have now been employed a year, and their pay increased." [1]

A few cautions are necessary. The charities of a large city often attract from the country those for whom there is no economic place. Our immigration laws have allowed many to come to America for whom there is no place, and charity has kept them alive here, knowing the while that they are forcing down the standard of living among our poor, and complicating the problem incalculably at every turn. But, as concerns interstate emigration, and the migration from country to city, charity should not be so helpless. It is within our power to refuse, by charitable aid, to settle the man who cannot settle himself in a community where he does not belong. It is often doing other workers a wrong to establish him and find work for him where he has no claim. The attractions of a large city are great enough without adding

[1] Thirteenth Report of Boston Associated Charities, p. 42.

any such artificial help to overcrowding. Our effort, on the contrary, should be to get back into country life those families that are found to be really fitted for it. Advertise in country papers, interest friends in the country in finding places for families, and do not fail to keep up communication either by letter or occasional visits with families so placed.[1]

One more caution. It helps a man to know that some one cares and will help him to find work; but it cripples him to let him feel that he can sit idle and let his friend do all the searching and worrying. "Send a man to find work, and go with him to a special place; but never go from place to place seeking it for him." Develop his resources, show an interest in all his efforts, and encourage him to renewed effort.

It has been claimed that only men and men of business experience can be successful friendly visitors where the head of the family is concerned; that, in matters of employment especially, a woman visitor is not capable of giving sound advice. It is undoubtedly true

[1] See "Charities Review," Vol. VI, pp. 402 *sq.*

that such work could be better done if more men, instead of contenting themselves with service on charitable boards, would take the trouble to become personally acquainted with a few poor families. This would be better for the boards and better for the men that are charitable trustees. But the woman visitor need not despair. It is true that she could do her work better, as will appear in this book, if she were in her own person a lawyer, a sanitary engineer, a trained cook, a kindergartner, and an expert financier; but she may be none of these things and still be a very good friendly visitor. When legal complications arise, she will go to some friend who is a lawyer; when the children get into trouble, she will consult a teacher, or an agent of the children's aid society, and, in the same way, the matter of employment will send her to a business man, or some one who can advise her, when her own store of experience is too scant. The poor man often has a mean opinion of the judgment of "charitable ladies," and this opinion has not always been without a degree of justification; but the visitor who takes the trouble to go on Sunday and get acquainted with the men folk, or makes occasion for them to come to her house from time to time, who proves herself, moreover, not without resource or common sense as emergencies arise, will soon overcome this prejudice and become the friend of every member of the family.

Collateral Readings: "The Settlement and Municipal Reform," James B. Reynolds in Proceedings of Twenty-third National Conference of Charities, pp. 138 *sq*. "Benevolent Features of Trades-Unions," John D. Flannigan in the same, pp. 154 *sq*. "The Ethical Basis of Municipal Corruption," Miss Jane Addams in "International Journal of Ethics," for April, 1898. "The Workers," Walter A. Wyckoff. "Working People and their Employers," Washington Gladden. "Problem of the Unemployed," Hobson. "The Unemployed," Geoffrey Drage. "Korbey's Fortune," William T. Elsing in "Scribner's," Vol. XVI, pp. 590 *sq*.

CHAPTER III

THE BREADWINNER AT HOME

We have considered the breadwinner as worker, neighbor, and citizen; we now turn to the breadwinner as husband and father. It has been said that the home is not only the true unit of society, but that it is the charitable unit as well, and that when we deal with anything less than a whole family, we deal with fractions. Much of our charitable work is still fractional. It not infrequently happens, for instance, that the members of one poor family will come in contact with dozens of charitable people representing many forms of charitable activity, and that none of these will ever have considered the family as a whole. The Sunday-school teacher, the kindergartner, the day nursery manager, the fresh air charity agent, the district nurse, the obstetric nurse, the church almoner, the city missionary, the relief agent, the head of the mothers' meeting, the guild teacher, the manager of the boys' brigade or girls' friendly, — all these will have touched the family at some point, but will never have taken the trouble to make a picture of the family life as a whole, and of the effect of their charity upon it. They may have assumed important responsibilities now and again, home responsibilities that belonged primarily to members of the family, and helped to hold the family together; but the chances are that they will none of them have worked continuously or thoroughly enough to learn from their blunders or to repair their mistakes.

I have mentioned home responsibilities. Let us consider, for a moment, what these are. They have an old-fashioned and conservative sound, but the fundamental facts of life are old-fashioned. The man is still the head of the normal family, and, as the head, still owes his best endeavor to secure for the other members of the family the means of subsistence. The wife's part in the family is to transform the means provided into a home. The children, for their part, should be teachable and obedient; and, as their own strength waxes and their parents' wanes, they should stand ready to provide for father and mother both the means of subsistence and the home environment. These are the prosaic but fundamental elements of home life, and, when they are lacking, neither the marriage ceremony, nor the sanctions of law and custom, can prevent the home from becoming a sham home, a breeding place of sin and social disorder.

It is my misfortune that, in attempting to meet the needs of those who visit the poor, I must dwell more upon the difficulties than upon the encouragements of such work. There are many poor homes where every essential element of home life exists. The home may be of the humblest sort, — it may be in one room, — but, to the best of his ability, the man is struggling to provide for his family; the woman is striving to make the little shelter homelike; and the children are learning that, out of the simplest elements, a certain measure of peace, orderliness and growth may be won. The home relation is right, and, though sickness, industrial depression, accident, or some other of the misfortunes that assail us from without may have made charitable relief necessary for a long time, the elements of successful charitable aid are there, because the home life works *with* the visitor to win back health and independence.

There is a deep satisfaction in protecting such families from the careless, patronizing charity of the thoughtless almsgiver, whose unsteady hand would give them a feast to-day and a famine to-morrow. There is deep satisfaction in coöperating with such families to conquer difficulties. There is a deeper satisfaction, however, in turning a sham home into a real one; in teaching the slatternly, irresponsible mother the pleasure of a cleanly, well-ordered home; in helping a man who has lost his sense of responsibility toward wife and children to regain it. Even at the risk of drawing a too gloomy picture, I dwell in this chapter, therefore, upon the husband and father who is either lazy or drunken or both.

The married vagabond has many characteristics of the single vagabond or tramp, though he is usually less enterprising. His is a type peculiar to our large cities, where political, industrial, and charitable conditions have helped to make him what he is. There is a sense in which he is not responsible for his faults; but there is a sense in which we are none of us responsible for ours, and when we are once permanently committed to this view of ourselves, there is no health in us. To treat the married vagabond as not responsible, is only to increase his irresponsibility.

"One man I know who has done hardly a stroke of work for years," says Mrs. Bosanquet; "during his wife's periodical confinements he goes off on the tramp, leaving her to take her chance of charity coming to the rescue, and returns when she can get to work again. I have known fathers who would send their hungry children to beg food from their neighbors, and then take it to eat themselves; and one I have known who would stop his children in the street and take their shoes from their feet to pawn for drink. The negative attitude of a man to his own family is an impossible one; if responsibility disappears, it will be replaced by brutality." [1]

And again, from the same book: "Take a case which is constantly recurring. A man has let himself drift into bad ways: he neglects his work, spends his money for drink, cares less and less about his family; the children become more and more neglected and starved. At last some charitable agency steps in. 'The man is hopeless,' it says, 'there is no question of relieving him of responsibility, for he has already lost all sense of that, and matters cannot be made worse by our interference. The children must not be allowed to suffer for their father's sins; we will feed and clothe and educate them, and so give them a chance of doing better than their parents.' All very well, if this were the only family; and we should all rush joyfully to the work of rescuing the little ones. But next door on either side are men with the same downward path so easy before them, and to a large extent restrained from entering upon it by the thought, 'What will become of the children?' This restraining

[1] "Rich and Poor," p. 105.

influence will break down much more rapidly for the knowledge that Smith's children are better cared for since he gave up the battle, and so the mischief spreads down the street like an epidemic." [1]

The method to be followed in dealing with the family of the married vagabond must depend upon circumstances, but it will usually be necessary to let him find out what the charitable community expects of him, and this he will hardly do unless the charitable withhold all aid except in the form of work. A visitor will not succeed in bringing this about until he has taken the trouble to find out what sources of relief are open to the family, and has persuaded each source to withhold relief. Visitors often hesitate to urge this radical measure, fearing that it will bring suffering upon the wife and children; but the plain fact is that the family of a lazy man must suffer, that no amount of material relief can prevent their suffering.

On this disputed point I venture to quote what I have written elsewhere: "Let us con-

[1] pp. 72 *sq.*

sider the chances that a married vagabond's children have of escaping suffering in a large city. . . . They are born into a world where the father is inconsiderate and abusive of the mother; where cleanliness, fresh air, and good food are not assured to them; where all the economic laws of the civilized world seem topsy-turvy; where things sometimes come miraculously, without any return for them in labor, and where they sometimes do not come at all. They are born, moreover, with diseased bodies, often with the taint of alcoholism in their veins; too often with some other inherited malady, such as epilepsy or unsound mind, as a direct result of parental excesses. How can we say that we 'do not let children suffer,' so long as alms keeps together thousands of these so-called homes in our large cities, and, worst of all, so long as into these homes thousands of helpless, unfortunate babies are born every year? If I were one of these same little ones, and could see what the charitable people were about, I should feel inclined to say: 'Ladies and gentlemen, you have supplied the doctor, and the nurse, and the fuel, and the sick diet; doubtless you mean it kindly, but I have been assisted into a world where you don't intend to give me a fair chance. You know that my father won't work for me, that my mother has no time to care for me, and that my brothers and sisters must fare worse than ever, now that there's one more mouth to feed. Moreover, my nerves are none of the strongest, and my body none of the stoutest. Unless you intend to do a great deal more for me, I'm sorry you didn't do less. Frankly, I don't thank you.'"[1]

Often when a man finds that charitable people are quite in earnest, that they really intend to place upon his shoulders the responsibility of his own family, he will bestir himself and go to work. He is not likely to stay and let his family starve. In fact, I have often found that the withholding of relief from the family of the married vagabond has the immediate effect of improving the material condition of the family — the man has either found work or left home. This method of being charitable requires courage, but if

[1] "Charities Review," Vol. VI, pp. 121 *sq.*

people would only see how wretchedness is perpetuated by the temporizing method, it would require courage to give small doles.

In many states there are laws for the punishment of the man that will not support his family. Some of these enactments are of very little use, but several of the New England states have effective laws.[1] When a complete cutting off of charitable supplies fails to bring a man to some sense of his duty, the visitor should try to have him punished by the courts. The evidence of one who has faithfully visited a family for a long time is very valuable in such cases, though conviction is often difficult to secure for lack of the wife's testimony. If the married vagabond that has been punished is still incurably lazy and irresponsible, the visitor should not allow his desire to reform the man to stand in the way of the best interests of the children, born and unborn. The wife's duty to her husband is a very sacred one, but so is her duty to her children. When

[1] See Proceedings of the Twenty-second National Conference of Charities and Correction, New Haven, 1895, pp. 514 *sq.*

all other measures fail, the home should be broken up.

Only those who have had wide charitable experience will be likely to consider this separation of man and wife justifiable. Says Mrs. Josephine Shaw Lowell: "I have not the slightest doubt that it is a *wrong*, and a great wrong, to give help to the family of a drunkard or an immoral man who will not support them. Unless the woman will remove her children from his influence, it should be understood that no public or private charity, and no charitable individual, has the right to help perpetuate and maintain such families as are brought forth by drunkards and vicious men and women."[1]

It is unnecessary to say that the advocates of separation as a last resort do not approve of divorce, which would only multiply sham homes. They recognize in certain cases "the sad fact of incurability," and are prepared to take courageous measures in order that the innocent may not suffer with the guilty.[2]

---

[1] "Public Relief and Private Charity," p. 105.

[2] See on this subject the Proceedings of the Twenty-fourth National Conference of Charities and Correction at Toronto, 1897, pp. 5 *sq.*

The following history of a Baltimore married vagabond will illustrate the need of separation in certain cases: Several years ago the Baltimore Charity Organization Society made the acquaintance of the family of a good-looking German shoemaker, who had married a plain, hard-working woman some years his senior. Soon after their marriage he began to neglect his work, and, depending more and more on his wife's exertions for his support, he took to drink. Child-bearing often incapacitated the wife for work, and church and charitable friends aided at such times. When the sixth child was a year old, he deserted his family for a while, but came back again, after having been in jail for disorderly conduct. The Charity Organization Society, seeing no chance of reforming the man, suggested that his wife leave him, but the German pastor strongly objected to any separation of man and wife, and nothing was done. A discouraging aspect of the situation was that the man taught his children to deceive the hard-working mother. When the seventh baby was born, and charity had supplied a registered nurse, baby linen, a doctor, fuel, and food, it was discovered that the man had sold the fuel supplied by the relief society, and had gone on a spree. He was a good workman, and could always have work when sober, but even when at work he neglected to provide properly for his family. Stung at last into active resistance, his wife had him arrested for non-support. While the man awaited trial, the Charity Organization Society removed his family, found work for the wife where she could keep three of her children, placed one with a relative, and two others temporarily in institutions. When he was released, he had no family to attract charitable aid, and was thrown, for the first time in many years, entirely upon his own resources.

Many good people may think that to deprive a man of family ties is to hasten his downfall; but what downfall could be more complete than the downfall of the man who not only permits his wife to support him, but abuses her and his children? In making this no longer possible we are sometimes doing the one thing that can be done to save him from spreading the contagion of his brutality, and so assuming a still heavier burden of sin.

There are many charitable visitors to whom the very thought of strong drink is so offensive, to whom everything connected with the saloon seems so brutal and degraded, that they are unable to make allowance for national, neighborhood, and family traditions in judging a man's habits. It sometimes happens that a whole family are condemned as "frauds" because they drink beer for dinner, or because the man of the house has been seen to enter a saloon. On no subject, perhaps, are charity workers so divided as on the question of how best to deal with the drink evil. Here, if anywhere, fanaticism is excusable, perhaps; but here, as everywhere, the friendly visitor must be on guard against personal prejudice and a hasty jumping at conclusions. "At night all cats are gray," says the old proverb, and it is only the benighted social reformer that thinks of all who drink as drunkards, and of all places where liquor is sold as dens of vice. The saloon is still the workingman's club, and, until some satisfactory substitute is found for it, all our denunciations will fail to banish it. It is none the less true that, of all personal habits, the drink habit stands next to licentiousness as a cause of poverty and degeneration.

"The problem of intemperance meets us in less than half the families that we know," says the Secretary of the Boston Associated Charities, "but it is that half which gives us the most concern. There are many ways of dealing with the drunkards and with their families, and the remedy must be separately chosen for each case. Some of our friends are impatient with all these partial remedies and will use none of them, waiting until they can sweep out of the State the alcohol which seems to them the whole cause of the trouble. But if it were all taken away to-morrow, I feel sure we should find this also only a partial remedy, and that the same want of self-control which makes men and women drunkards would drive some of them to-morrow to other and perhaps worse stimulants. So, while I hope and believe that slowly and steadily the sentiment of individuals is growing toward total abstinence, and that in the course of years, generations, perhaps, it will become the law of the State, I believe in working man to man and woman to woman in building up and strengthening character as the chief safeguard against so great an evil." [1]

The first thing, in dealing with an individual case of drunkenness, is to find out its history. Is it the cause of poverty and misfortune, or have poverty and misfortune caused it? Is there an inherited tendency to drink, or did the habit originate in some other bad personal habit? Is bad health the cause? Has unhealthy or dangerous employment anything to do with it? Is bad home cooking one of the causes? Some one has said that the best temperance lecturer is the properly filled dinner-pail. Worry from lack of work, and the need of some warm stimulant after exposure, are frequent causes; and they are both removable with friendly help. A man who is honestly trying to break himself of the drink habit

[1] Miss Z. D. Smith in Report of Union Relief Association of Springfield, Mass., 1887.

deserves all the patience, sympathy, and resourcefulness at our command.

When a man is sensitive and proud, the visitor can often be most helpful by simply showing his sympathy. "A travelling salesman who became addicted to drink lost a good situation through this habit. He had a wife and seven children, all the children being too young to earn anything. The wife was very brave and supported the family as long as she was able. When the case came to the Charity Organization Society the rent was in arrears and the landlord threatening. We sent a gentleman as our friendly visitor in the case, and after great persistence and repeated failures he succeeded in keeping the head of the family sober for a few days. The man was proud, and much hurt at having to accept charity, but his family was suffering, and there was no alternative. The aid was provided in so delicate a manner that the man's heart was touched, and he became very grateful to the visitor for his unflagging and kindly interest. They spent their evenings together frequently. The man began to drink less, at last stopped altogether, and now has secured permanent work and is doing well." [1]

There is diversity of opinion as to the value of pledges. It would seem unwise, however, when a man has broken a pledge, to encourage him to renew it. Let him try a promise to himself, and prove that he can be a man without artificial props.

In more stubborn cases the law must be invoked. Sometimes it is well to try several remedies at once, asking the police to threaten arrest, following this up at once with an invitation to join some temperance society (preferably one connected with the man's church), and trying at the same time to substitute some new interest. Milder measures failing, it will sometimes be necessary to cut off all supplies of relief, and, this again failing, to take steps to protect wife and children from the brutalizing influence of the man by breaking up the home.

There are many causes of the drink evil, as I have tried to show, but, after every allowance has been made, the chief cause will often be found in the selfishness of the human heart.

[1] "Charities Record," Baltimore, Vol. I, No. 1.

There are men who do not care to be cured of drunkenness, who feel no shame for the misery and degradation brought upon their families. Here again the "sad fact of incurability" must be recognized. It is folly to let such men discover that, through our charitable interest in their families, we will either directly or indirectly pay their whiskey bills, or will assume the burdens that they deliberately shirk. A Committee on Intemperance, reporting to the Ward VIII. Conference of the Boston Associated Charities in 1886, called attention to this aspect of the question. "The committee, however, say that, in their opinion, the question of moral responsibility on the part of the intemperate, and also, in its degree, on the part of those who, by gifts or other aid, make intemperance easy, is too much lost sight of ; and they believe that the refusal of all aid to the families of drunkards, outside the almshouse, unless in exceptional cases, would bring about a better state of opinion and a juster sense of responsibility. The committee add that it will be almost impossible to make kind-hearted people believe this, since they are more moved by the sight of present suffering than by the hope of future permanent improvement, to secure which some measure of present suffering may be necessary."[1]

Collateral Readings: "An Adventure in Philanthropy," Edwin C. Martin in "Scribner's," Vol. XI, pp. 230 *sq*. "Charity and Home Making," the present writer in "Charities Review," Vol. VI, No. 2. "Married Vagabonds," the same, in Proceedings of Twenty-second National Conference of Charities, pp. 514 *sq*. "Drunkards' Families," Rev. W. F. Slocum in Proceedings of Fifteenth National Conference of Charities, pp. 131 *sq*. "The Social Value of the Saloon," E. C. Moore in "American Journal of Sociology," Vol. III, No. 1. "Substitutes for the Saloon," F. G. Peabody in "Forum" for July, 1896. "Law and Drink," Frederick H. Wines in "Charities Review," Vol. VII, Nos. 3 and 4.

[1] Seventh Report of Boston Associated Charities, p. 39.

CHAPTER IV

THE HOMEMAKER

THE wife brings us to another aspect of the home, though it cannot be too often repeated that all aspects are so inextricably interwoven that they must be considered together. When the wife takes the means provided, the raw material from which a home is to be made, she engages in a very complicated form of manufacture, including in its processes the buying, preparation, and serving of food, the care of the household possessions, the buying, making, and care of clothing, the training of children, and many minor departments. These are only processes, however, and, unless the maker have an ideal picture in her mind of what a home should be, neither some nor all of these processes will make a home.

In dealing with the homemaker, the friendly visitor becomes more directly a teacher, though it is often necessary that she should first be a learner. The agent of a New York charity tells of a friendly visitor who was consulted by the agent about a family applying for relief. They were found to have an income of $20.00 a week. "Well," said the visitor, "that is very little money on which to raise a family." The agent felt that this visitor had not only a great deal to learn, but a great deal to unlearn.

Not every visitor is skilled in buying and preparing food, or in arranging a household budget, and the visitor that is skilful in doing this on one scale of expenditure may be quite ignorant and helpless in dealing with another and much smaller scale. One who is really in earnest, however, in the desire to help another, will never give up because there are difficulties to overcome. The visitor may not know, but as compared with the homemaker in a poor family, has far more time and a greater facility, perhaps, in learning. The visitor's best teachers are friends that have had experience, and the poor themselves. One can learn a great deal from the more frugal and industrious of the very poor, and these are proud to explain their small economies, when our reasons for wishing to learn are made clear to them.

Lacking these teachers, there are books, though books have the disadvantage of never meeting the needs of any one locality. Variations of climate, custom, and the local markets make specific suggestions about buying difficult. For this reason I shall not attempt to go into detail, but suggest that, as our relations with our poor friends should be as natural as possible, when we do not know anything, it is always best to frankly say so, and then think out with them some way of learning. For instance, it would be natural enough for a visitor to say to the homemaker: "We both feel that there is a lot to learn about the best way of buying and preparing food. I have an acquaintance that has made a study of the subject, and, with your permission, I am going to bring her here, to give us both some suggestions."

Scientific dietaries have been prepared with a view to teaching the poor to use nutritious and economical foods. Professor J. J. Atwater, Edward Atkinson, Mrs. Juliet Corson, and Mrs. Mary Hinman Abel are authorities on this subject. The Bureau of Associated Charities, Orange, N. J., publishes a leaflet on foods, prepared by Mrs. S. E. Tenney of Brooklyn. Taking Orange prices, a dietary is given for a family of six (man, wife, and four children), at a cost of $3.31 per week. In urging changes in diet upon poor families, it is first necessary to become well acquainted with the families, and, even then, to introduce any innovations slowly, one thing at a time. A friendly visitor in Baltimore has tried the plan of meeting her friends in market, and pointing out to them the best cuts of meat, the best place to buy vegetables, etc. But her greatest success in introducing new dishes has been through the children. She has been wise enough to secure the coöperation of her cook, and, by inviting the children into her own kitchen on Saturday mornings, has taught them the best way to prepare simple dishes. She finds that scientific dietaries too often ignore the tastes and prejudices of the poor. It is best to begin by teaching them to prepare well the things that they like. If they are devoted to strong tea, for instance, we can teach them first of all that it should not boil on the stove all day.

When we are dealing with questions of taste, whether in manners, diet, clothing, or household decoration, we cannot afford to take the attitude of the Rev. Mr. Honeythunder, "Come up and be blessed, or I'll knock you down!" We may find a preference for cheap finery very exasperating, but our own example is far more likely to be followed in the long run if we do not insist upon it too much at first. Begin by teaching the homemaker to mend and keep the clothing in good order, and give her some of your own experience as to which materials wear the best.

One of the important items of expenditure is fuel, and the first thing to find out under this head is whether kerosene or any other inflammable fluid is ever used to start the fire. Experienced housekeepers say that it is good economy to have stoves with small gratings and then buy a good grade of pea coal, which, if carefully used, is cheaper and quite as economical as more expensive grades. The poor often prefer expensive, free-burning coals because they are little trouble. A practical engineer says that, in burning pea coal, the fire must be kept clean, not by violent shaking, but by a straight poker used on the bottom of the fire only. Remove clinkers through the top. Add coal in small quantities, and, when not using the fire, give it a good cleaning at the bottom, spread enough coal to make about three inches of fuel in all, put on the draught until kindled, add four inches of fresh coal, allowing the draught to remain on until the gas is burned off, then shut the bottom draughts, take the lids half-way off, and open the top slide, if the stove has one.

In many of the homes into which visitors go, cleanliness seems the greatest lack. Sometimes the mother has lost heart; sometimes she has never known what cleanliness was. Tact is necessary here to avoid hurting the feelings of our poor friends, though some are far more sensitive than others. The Boston woman whose visitor sent soap, scrubbing brushes, mop, and pail, with the message that she was coming on the morrow to use them, took this very broad hint and made the home tidy for the first time in many months, but it is unnecessary to say that all poor people could not be dealt with in this way. One visitor went, when she knew the mother would be absent, and helped the children to clean the house. Another found that, if the family knew she was coming, the home was set in order; so she was careful for a time to come at stated intervals, then tried irregular visits, and was finally rewarded by finding the home presentable at all times.

"Mr. William D. Howells, who during his recent residence in Boston gave much of his valuable time as a visitor for the Associated Charities, was amused one day to be told, on knocking at the door of a house where he had studiously endeavored to inspire a sense of cleanliness, that he could not come in, as the floor had just been washed and he might soil it again."[1]

Housecleaning seasons are not always observed in poor homes. The visitor can call attention to the value of whitewash as a cleaning agent, and if once taught to do it, the children take pleasure in putting it on.

---

[1] Mrs. Roger Wolcott in Proceedings of International Congress of Charities at Chicago, Volume on "Organization of Charities," p. 110.

It is not merely as the adviser about household matters that the visitor can be helpful to the homemaker. Many women in poor neighborhoods lead starved, sordid lives, and long for genuine friendliness and sympathy. A friend who would be helpful to them must exercise the same self-restraint that our own friends exercise with us. The friends who encourage us to exaggerate our troubles and difficulties are not our best friends: theirs is a friendship that tends to weaken our moral fibre. But the sympathy that the poor need and all of us need is the sympathy that makes us feel stronger, the sympathy that is farthest removed from sentimentality. We should be willing to listen patiently to the homemaker's troubles, and should strive to see the world from her point of view, but at the same time we should help her to take a cheerful and courageous tone. One unfailing help, when our poor friends dwell too much upon their own troubles, is to tell them ours. Here, too, indirect suggestion is powerful. The wife, in her attitude toward husband and children, will unconsciously imitate our own attitude toward them. As Miss Jane Addams says, if the visitor kisses the baby and makes much of it, the mother will do the same. A Baltimore visitor has cured one tired woman of scolding her husband in season and out of season by diverting her attention to other things, and by seeking her coöperation in plans for improving the man's habits.

A New York visitor tells of a woman living in a two-room tenement who is regarded as a marvel by her husband's friends because she makes a point of having a specially good meal one night in the week, and it is understood that her husband can bring his friends home to supper on that night without giving her warning. The home is very humble, but she has learned the wisdom of making it a real home for her husband, and one that he can be proud of.

So far, I have ignored the fact that, in the poor home, the woman is often the breadwinner as well as the homemaker. I wish it were possible to ignore the further fact that charitable visitors, finding it difficult to get work for the man or finding him disinclined to take it, will bestir themselves to get work for the woman instead. One of the few rules which it is safe to follow blindly is the rule that we should not encourage any woman to become the breadwinner who has an able-bodied, unemployed man in the house. "Only harm can result," says Mrs. Lowell, "if efforts are made to induce the woman to leave her home daily for work."

Where the breadwinner is disabled, or the woman is a deserted wife or widow, work is, of course, necessary. We must distinguish, however, between the deserted wife and the wife whose husband chronically deserts her, until her condition attracts the charitable help that he returns to share. Widows with children belong to a class with which charity has dealt too harshly in the past. When the woman is incapable of supporting all her children, and this is usually the case, charity has either allowed her family to depend upon insufficient doles and so drift into beggary, or else has put all the children in orphanages. If the mother is a good mother, capable with help of rearing her children to independence and self-support, this latter is not only a cruel but a wasteful method. As charity becomes more discriminating and resourceful, it will be possible to organize pensions for widows of this class, though these pensions will need the careful oversight of a visitor, who should see that the children are taught to bear the family burden as they become older.

There is great diversity of opinion about the value of mothers' meetings for women whose home duties prevent them from attending church on Sunday. If these meetings confined themselves to providing what the church service provides, — a chance for spiritual uplifting and refreshment, — there could be no possible objection to them; but, unfortunately, many mothers' meetings strive to attract and hold members by such small devices as paying them for very bad sewing, or making small gifts, or selling things below cost. These attractions, small as they are, lead many women to neglect their home duties, and it is no unusual thing for one woman to belong to three mothers' meetings of three different denominations, which take her away from home three afternoons in the week. The atmosphere of patronage and "sprinkling charity" that is so common in these meetings, distinctly lowers the self-respect of the women; before very long they learn to write begging notes or send begging messages to "the ladies" in charge, and the place that should be for them a source of spiritual strength becomes merely a source of supplies.

Collateral Readings: "The Lustig's" and "Corinna's Fiametta," Mrs. Schuyler Van Rensselaer in "One Man who was Content and Other Stories." "Practical Sanitary and Economic Cooking" (adapted to persons of moderate and small means), Mrs. Mary Hinman Abel, published by American Public Health Association, Rochester, N.Y. "Foods: Nutritive Value and Cost," by W. O. Atwater in Farmer's Bulletin No. 23 of United States Department of Agriculture. "Dietary Studies in New York City," W. O. Atwater and Charles D. Woods in Bulletin No. 46 of United States Department of Agriculture. The Health Department of New York City will soon publish leaflets prepared by experts, which will contain simple directions about buying and preparing food. "The Le Play Method of Social Observation," "American Journal of Sociology," Vol. II, No. 1. "Treatment of Widows and Dependent Children," Mrs. L. Wolcott in Proceedings of Fifteenth National Conference of Charities, pp. 137 *sq*. "Girls in a Factory Valley," Mrs. Lillie B. Chace Wyman in "Atlantic," Vol. LXXVIII, pp. 391 *sq*. and 506 *sq*.

CHAPTER V

THE CHILDREN

THE visitor in the homes of the poor whose chief concern is with questions of material relief often overlooks the children entirely, unless they are large enough to be forced into the labor market and made to contribute toward the family income. In charity meetings, where visitors get together to discuss the difficulties of individual families, it will often happen that the children are not mentioned. On the other hand, there is a large class of charity workers who concern themselves with the children only, and a strongly marked tendency of modern charity is to treat the children of the poor quite apart from and without any relation to their home life. "We constantly hear it said," writes Mrs. James Putnam, "that we cannot help the older ones, but that we must save the children. It seems clear to me that to help one without the other is usually an impossible task. Their interests are too closely bound together."[1]

There is always danger, in our eagerness to help the children, that we may only encourage parents to shirk their duty. Take the admirable charities known as day nurseries. If care is not taken to exclude all except the children of widows, or of women whose husbands are disabled, these will only encourage laziness in the husband, and help to bring about that unwholesome condition in which the wife is breadwinner, homemaker, and childbearer.

The first thing that a visitor should observe in a family where there is a baby is whether the child is nursed too many months and too often. A child should not be nursed during the night after it is six months old. Solid food is usually given too soon; tea and coffee are often given before the child is a year old, and to these is added "anything on the table."

[1] Proceedings of Fifteenth National Conference of Charities, 1887, p. 152.

For the children's sake, the visitor should be very observant. It is difficult, at first, to find out how they are fed, bathed, and clothed, and whether they go to bed early, in clean beds and ventilated rooms; but one can learn more by observation than by direct questions. Ask to see the baby bathed, and notice the condition of its scalp and skin. If in any doubt, it is always best to consult a doctor; do not allow your ignorance to make you a non-conductor. Learn how to sterilize milk, and teach the mother; show her the importance of feeding at regular intervals, and impress upon her that small children should never have stimulants, greasy food, green fruit, or cakes, nuts, and candies.

In summer, the baby should have frequent airings in the nearest park, and, in case of sickness, the visitor should know how to use the children's sanitariums, floating hospitals, free excursions or other charities provided for sick children. For the older children it will be possible to procure a country holiday through the fresh air society or the children's country homes that are provided within easy distance of all our large cities. Or, better still, the visitor may know some one in the country, or may have a summer home there, where the little ones can be entertained. Any one who has once realized how important it is that every growing child should know and love the country, will gladly put up with some personal inconvenience to give this knowledge to the little folk in the family he visits.

As soon as the children are old enough, connection should be made with the nearest kindergarten, or if, unfortunately, there is no kindergarten near enough, the visitor should learn some of the kindergarten games and occupations, and teach the children. When the children go to the public schools, the visitor should make the acquaintance of their teacher.

"One of our visitors went for two years to visit a widow and her children without feeling that she accomplished anything, though the intercourse was pleasant enough in itself. Then she heard that the girl of thirteen was having trouble in school and was in danger of being expelled. She went to see the teacher.

The girl was always well dressed, and the teacher had no idea she was a poor girl. After seeing the visitor the teacher touched the girl at last by talking with her of the sacrifices her mother had made for her education, and urging her to do her part, that her mother's hard work might not be in vain. In this way she persuaded the girl to good behavior and kept her in school — all because some one had visited the family for a year or two and could speak confidently of their condition and character." [1]

No one can work among the poor in their homes without realizing the need of compulsory education laws. There are still people here and there who talk about the danger of educating the poor "above their station," but those who know the poor in our large cities from actual contact feel that over-education is the very least of the dangers that beset them. The lack of adequate school accommodations, making it impossible to punish truancy, is a much greater danger, and, in some States, the absence of any compulsory education law

[1] Miss Z. D. Smith.

makes the child the easy victim of trade conditions and of parental greed. The visitor should never permit the desire to increase the family income to blind him to the fact that the physical, mental, and moral welfare of the child is seriously endangered by wage-earning. Where there is a compulsory education law, he should coöperate with the truant officers in securing its enforcement; where there is no such law, every influence should be brought to bear upon parents to keep children in school. The Hebrew Benevolent Society of Detroit refuses aid to families in which the children are kept from school, and all our relief agencies, churches included, would do well to adopt this rule.

Some of the most intelligent and devoted workers in child-saving agencies have sounded the note of warning on the subject of children wage-earners. "The fact," says Mrs. Anna Garlin Spencer, "that the world of industry has found out and established methods of labor which can utilize the work of children to profit, gives to that world of industry, as an upper and a nether millstone, the greed of employers and the cupidity and poverty of parents, between which the life of the child is often ground to powder."[1] And Mrs. Florence Kelley, writing from her experience as a factory inspector in Illinois, says: "I do not mean that every boy is usually ruined by his work, but I do mean that, the earlier the child goes to work, the greater the probability of ruin. I mean, too, that there is to be gained, from a scientific study of the working child, an irradiating side-light upon the tramp question, the unemployed question, and the whole ramifying question of the juvenile offender. . . . One reason that immigrants cling so closely to the great cities is that they find there far more opportunity to get money for their children's work. There is probably no one means of dispersing the disastrously growing colonies of our great cities so simple and effective as this one, of depriving the children of their immediate cash value."[2]

[1] Proceedings of International Congress of Charities, Chicago, 1893. Volume on "Care of Children," p. 7.

[2] Proceedings of Twenty-third National Conference of Charities, 1896, p. 164.

Another hindrance to the proper education of the children is the habit of keeping them from school to run errands, to carry their fathers' dinners, or to help with the housework. The girls are often taken away from school very early for trivial reasons.

Recent developments in child study show that many of the moral and mental obliquities of children may be traced to physical defects. In dealing with wayward and dull children, the visitor should bear this fact in mind, and, either by observation or by the help of a physician, discover wherein the child is defective. The sooner a defect is discovered, the easier it will be to cure it, and for this reason the visitor should learn to apply simple tests for defective sight and hearing.

In a very instructive article, which every visitor should read, on "Child Study,"[1] Professor Krohn says that "dull" children suffer from defective hearing in ninety-nine out of one hundred cases. He tells of one girl in a class who failed to answer correctly, and was said by the teacher to be the most stupid child in the

[1] "Charities Review," Vol. VI, pp. 433 *sq.*

school. "After the class was dismissed, I told the teacher that I did not believe that the little girl was intellectually stupid; that there was probably some physical defect clogging the pathway to her active little brain; and I requested an opportunity to talk to the child at recess, when I found that she could not hear my stop-watch tick until it was within nine inches of her right ear, and eleven inches of her left ear. The average child, under the same local conditions, can hear the same watch tick at a distance of twenty-one feet. How could the poor child answer correctly when she could not hear what was asked? Every answer was a mere guess. After a time any child would become stupid under such conditions, believing it of no use to attempt to answer at all. This little girl was, at my suggestion, given a seat not far from the teacher's desk and especial pains was afterward taken to speak distinctly to her. . . . She has since manifested such marked improvement that, at the close of the last school year, she ranked second in her class."

In puzzling cases of waywardness, the visitor

should seek the advice of the agent of the local children's aid society, who is often an expert, and glad to help one who is in earnest in such work. The Report of the Boston Children's Aid Society for 1896,[1] cites two cases of truancy due to physical defects. One was a girl of ten years, whose eyes were found to be defective. After fitting her with proper glasses, the Society's agent had her returned to school. Another was a boy of eight, with a slight impediment in his speech. No one had noticed that his schoolmates teased the child, until he told the agent. After the boy's teacher had been seen, there was no more laughing and no more truancy.

Massachusetts has an excellent system of placing juvenile offenders on probation for a first offence. This same report contains illustrations of the work of the Children's Aid Society's probation officer. "A boy, fifteen years of age, already on informal probation, and apparently doing fairly well, was suddenly brought into court, charged with breaking and entering his employer's shop at night. On

[1] pp. 13 *sq.*

account of his past good character, he was put on probation by the court under our agent's care. He told Mr. Lawrence that he got into this criminal state of mind by bad reading and by attending low theatrical performances. With the aid of the boy's Sunday-school teacher he has been encouraged to do his best, and is now working regularly, taking good books from the Public Library, and is doing very well."

The charitable are only beginning to discover the importance of such personal and preventive work among children, founded upon an intimate knowledge of their habits and character. Such work must be done in large measure by volunteers, and the friendly visitor's relations to poor families render him specially fit for the service. The illustration just given emphasizes the importance of guiding a child's reading. It is not enough to teach the children to use the Public Library; we should know what they are reading and teach them to enjoy the right books. An admirable system of lending libraries having this object in view has been established by the Boston Children's Aid Society. These little Home Libraries in small hanging book cases are placed in certain homes in poor neighborhoods, and the visitor in charge of a library meets at regular intervals a group of children of the neighborhood who form the library circle, explaining the books to them, playing games, and getting well acquainted. A friendly visitor might easily establish such a library in any poor neighborhood; the details of the plan may be had upon application to the Children's Aid Society.

Training in citizenship must not be overlooked. Our boys and girls should know more about our country than their parents can teach them. The publications of the Patriotic League, 230 W. 13th St., New York, will be found very useful. The League issues a Young Citizens' Catechism and a monthly journal, "Our Country." The Sunday-school is another help to the visitor, and it is well to know not only the public-school teacher, but the Sunday-school teacher, whose coöperation should be sought in any plans for the children's welfare. One Sunday-school is a help, but two or more Sunday-schools for one child are thoroughly demoralizing, and we should do our best to discourage any child in whom we are interested from going to more than one.

It too often happens that children are sent by their parents to several churches with the deliberate purpose of making profitable charitable connections. This habit of thrusting the children forward to excite sympathy, of sending them to ask help of teachers, clergymen, and charity agents, is so obviously bad for the children that one wonders how the charitable can ever have permitted it to become so general. Children should never be permitted to deliver begging notes and messages from a family in which there is an able-bodied adult.

Of all charitable practices that help to manufacture misery and vice, the practice of giving to child-beggars on the street is the most pernicious. One boy who has become a skilful beggar teaches another, and first the money goes for candy and cigarettes, then for gambling and low theatres. The next step is petty thieving, the next burglary, and then follow commitment to a reformatory, which often fails to reform, and, later, a criminal career. I have seen children travel this road so often that it is difficult to speak without bitterness of the unthinking alms that led them into temptation. Sometimes parents connive at child-begging, but often they know nothing of it until the children have grown incorrigible. A strict enforcement of the laws against child-begging is very difficult until every one is convinced of the cruelty of giving money to unknown children on the street or at the door.

It sometimes becomes the visitor's painful duty to protect children from cruelty, criminal neglect, or immorality by legal removal from their parents' control. Here a society for the protection of children will often render valuable assistance. Such a society is likely to be hampered in its work by the unwillingness of charitable visitors to tell what they know in court. Sometimes this is due to timidity, and sometimes to a fear of losing influence in the neighborhood. Clergymen have been known to refuse their testimony for this latter reason. The friendly visitor, whose interest is centred in only one family in the neighborhood, need not be so cautious, and his continuous visiting, extending over many months, makes his testimony very valuable. No fear of losing influence with other members of the family should prevent him from speaking out where a child's future is at stake. Just a few months more in evil surroundings may mean moral death to the child, and neighbors are notoriously unwilling to tell what they know.

It is impossible to enter here upon the vexed question of the relative merits of boarding-out dependent children, of placing them without pay in country homes, or of committing them to the care of institutions, though I cannot refrain from quoting, in passing, the opinion of Miss Mason, for twelve years an English government inspector of boarded-out children, that "well carried out, boarding-out may be the best way of caring for dependent children; ill carried out, it may be the worst." There is a very foolish saying that the worst home is better than the best institution, but no one who knows how bad a home can be or how good an institution can be will venture beyond the statement that, other things being equal, a home is certainly better than an institution. The friendly visitor should make himself familiar with what has been written on this subject, and should be prepared, in any given case, to make the wisest selection of a home that local conditions make possible, always remembering, of course, that his responsibility does not end here; that he should continue to visit the child, if it be placed within visiting distance.

The visitor should also be familiar with the local laws for the protection of children. These usually include laws against child-begging; against selling liquor and tobacco to minors; against the employment of children as pedlers, public singers, dancers, etc.; against the employment of children under a certain age for more than a specified number of hours (or prohibiting their employment entirely); and against the abduction or harboring of female minors for immoral purposes.

What, above the mastery of all these details,

should be the visitor's clear aim? To see to it that the children are better off than their parents were, and are saved from the pitfalls into which the latter have fallen; that the boys are better equipped to become breadwinners, and the girls to become homemakers. The training given in our public schools will often seem very inadequate, and some of us look forward to the day when every boy and girl between the ages of six and sixteen shall be trained to use hand and brain, when manual training shall be part of the daily instruction of every school course. Until this day comes, the visitor must make use of such aids as evening classes in boys' and girls' clubs, people's institutes, and Christian associations. A child's capabilities should be studied and every encouragement given to his small ambitions.

But the best help, after all, is in the personal influence that the visitor can acquire over the growing child. When we think what personal influence has done in our own lives, how it has moulded our convictions, our tastes, our very manner of speech, even, we should not despair of the children, if we can attach them to us and give them a new and better outlook upon life. The time when we can be of the greatest help to them is during the disorganized period that comes between the school days and the settling down in life. Many a young life has gone to wreck for lack of a guiding hand at this time, for lack of a friend to make suggestions about employment, companions, amusements, and home relations. The failure of philanthropy to make any adequate provision for this critical period accounts, in part, for the large number of married vagabonds in our great cities.

Collateral Readings: On care of infants see leaflets of local Boards of Health. "The Working Child," Florence Kelley in Proceedings of Twenty-third National Conference of Charities, pp. 161 *sq*. "The Working Boy," the same in "American Journal of Sociology," Vol. II, No. 3. "Child Labor," W. F. Willoughby and Clare de Graffenreid in publications of American Economic Association. "Influence of Manual Training on Character," Felix Adler in Proceedings of Fifteenth National Conference of Charities, pp. 272 *sq*. "Children of the Road," Josiah Flynt in "Atlantic," January, 1896. "Family Life for Dependent and Wayward Children," Homer Folks, volume on "Care of Children" in Proceedings of International Congress of Charities at Chicago, pp. 69 *sq*. Story of "The Child's

Mother," in Mrs. Margaret Deland's "Old Chester Tales."
"The Wisdom of Fools," Mrs. Margaret Deland (see, for
difficulties in reclaiming girls, the story entitled "The Law
and the Gospel"). Reports of Conventions of Working
Girls' Societies at Boston, 1894, and Philadelphia, 1897.
For pamphlets on School Savings Banks apply to J. H.
Thiry, Long Island City, N.Y.

CHAPTER VI

HEALTH

About one-fourth of all the poverty that has come within the scope of charitable investigation is directly caused by sickness. "In both American and English experience," writes Warner, "the percentage attributable to this cause sinks but once slightly below fifteen and never quite reaches thirty. The average is between twenty and twenty-five. This is one of the most significant facts brought out by these tables [of the statistical causes of poverty]. It is not one which the author anticipated when the collection of statistics began; and yet it has been confirmed and reconfirmed in so many ways that the conclusion seems inevitable that the figures set forth real and important facts. Personal acquaintance with the destitute classes has further convinced him that most of the causes of poverty result from or result in a weakened physical and mental constitution, often merging into actual disease." [1]

This fact gives added importance to all the efforts of modern charity to secure improved dwellings, open spaces, cheap baths, and better municipal sanitation for the poor. But improvement in these matters cannot come entirely from without; "the model tenement implies a model tenant." As a London authority puts it: "The condition of the house may degrade its occupants. The careless life and habits of the occupants will spoil the house, and make it filthy and unhealthy." The friendly visitor should try to make the family healthily discontented with unsanitary surroundings, and so prepare them for better quarters. Removing families from unfit tenements is not enough, however, if these tenements are almost immediately reoccupied. Their condition should be reported to the Board of Health, and, if condemned, we should see that no one else is permitted to move into them.

I have often noticed that charity agents,

[1] "American Charities," p. 40.

who work habitually in poor neighborhoods, get so accustomed to bad sanitary conditions that they hardly notice them. Volunteer workers are not so likely to fall into this error, though it is possible for volunteers to be very unobservant. They often feel that things are all wrong, without being able to state the specific difficulties. An observant visitor will learn the condition of the cellar, walls, yard, plumbing, and outhouses; will learn to take the cubic contents of a room in order to find out the air space for each sleeper; will learn the family method of garbage disposal; will see how the rooms are ventilated; and will learn all these things without asking many questions. Dampness is a very common cause of sickness; when the children cough it is a very simple matter to ask about the cellar, and even get permission to see it.

The prejudice against fresh air, especially night air, is a difficult one to overcome. One mother, who kept her children scrupulously clean, could never understand the value of fresh air until a visitor explained to her how air was polluted by the soiled air that we breathed out, just as water was polluted when we washed our hands in it. When the children breathed this soiled air in again it made them "dirty inside"; and this homely statement left such an unpleasant picture in the mother's mind that her rooms were always well ventilated afterward.

It is difficult to ventilate a small room without making a draft, but, next to the chimney, the upper sash is the simplest ventilator, and should not be immovable, as it is in many small houses. A board about five inches wide under the lower sash will make a current of air between the upper and lower sashes, and, better still, two pieces of elbow pipe with dampers, fixed in the board, will throw a good current of air upward into the room. Another ventilator can be made by tacking a strip of loosely woven material to the upper sash and to the top of the window-frame. When the upper sash is dropped, the stuff is drawn taut over the opening, and, while permitting air to pass through, breaks the current.

Equal in importance with fresh air inside the house is exercise out of doors. I was shocked some years ago to find that, of six Sunday-school boys who went with me on a little trip to our largest city park, five had never been there before. This had not been due to lack of time or money, though they had very little of either; but its sole cause had been lack of enterprise.

There is an impatient and popular saying that soap and water are cheap; like many other popular sayings, it is only half true. Personal cleanliness is rather expensive when one takes into account the time, energy, and frequent changes of clothing required to keep the body daintily clean. Visitors should realize this in any effort to introduce a higher standard of personal neatness, and should not be impatient when they do not immediately succeed. Cleanliness and health are so nearly related, however, that the effort is very well worth making. A visitor who hesitated to complain to a mother about her little girl's neglected condition, borrowed the child to spend the day, and brought her home at night sweet, clean, and rosy, with her hair well brushed and curled. The hint was taken.

It would be very unfortunate for the visitor to be an alarmist, for there are imaginary invalids among the poor as well as elsewhere, but more frequently the poor neglect the earlier symptoms of sickness altogether, or else dose themselves with patent medicines. The quack doctors who advertise in the daily papers draw much of their custom from the very poor, who are also large consumers of cure-alls and proprietary medicines. We have seen how children's physical defects can pass unnoticed at home, and this is the case in a less degree with the defects and ailments of adults. The very cheap grade of medical service that is sometimes given by regular practitioners in poor neighborhoods has a tendency to discourage the poor from taking sickness in time. The visitor can help them to procure better medical service at reasonable charges or, when necessary, without charge. The grade of service in dispensaries varies greatly, but the medical advice and directions given there with the medicines can be made far more useful if the visitor will go with the patient and see that the directions are understood and carried out. Often no adult in the family can spare the time to go with a sick child to the dispensary. Here, too, the visitor's service will be helpful. In cases of contagious disease, see that the Board of Health is notified promptly.

Other things being equal, an acute case of illness can usually be better and more economically cared for in a hospital than in a poor home. In fact, although hospitals were intended originally for the destitute sick, the practice of sending well-to-do patients there is rapidly spreading. The prejudice against hospitals, still so general among the poor, is a survival from a time when hospital care was far less humane than now. If the visitor has ever been a patient in a hospital, and can tell his own experience or the experiences of friends, or if he happens to know some of the doctors or nurses, and promises to see them about his poor friend, the prejudice can often be overcome. The dread of the untried and the unknown is natural enough, and yet it will happen now and then that hospital care is so clearly the best thing that nothing can take the place of it, and suffering and loss will be entailed upon the family by their refusal to let the sick member go. In such cases charitable people may be justified in helping the family to a right decision by withholding all relief.

The prejudice against hospitals is strong in the negro race. In the first family I ever visited the mother, a colored woman, had been bedridden for thirteen months. According to her own account she had been "conjured," and at first the mention of a hospital made her hysterical. She consented to let a doctor, who was a friend of mine, see her, and he pronounced her disease sciatic rheumatism. He said she could never get well at home with four small, noisy children, and, besides, the walls of her house were damp. After two months of persuading, I got the mother into a hospital and the family moved into a dry house. Among the arguments that won her were my own acquaintance with the hospital nurses, and my promise to visit her frequently while there; and my further promise to see that the children were well cared for while she was away. But the argument that tipped the scale was the promise to take her away to the hospital in a carriage with two horses.

Among the cases in which hospital care is not practicable are those of chronic invalids, of patients too sick to be moved, and of patients able to be treated as "out-patients" in the dispensaries. Confinement cases, where there are children in the family who must be placed temporarily in institutions if the mother leaves home, are best treated in the home. There are societies that provide a nurse and baby-linen at such times. Some families are so degraded that they look forward to times of confinement as times of plenty (see family cited on p. 55), and in these cases nothing but hospital care should be offered, while we place the children temporarily in institutions or with neighbors. For the destitute sick outside of hospitals, district nurses are now provided in many cities. When these nurses are careful to instruct well members of the household in the care of the sick, their influence is especially helpful, and they are often able not only to relieve suffering, but to raise the standard of living in the home. Diet kitchens, supplying food specially prepared for the sick either free or at a nominal cost, are also found in many of our cities.

With all the charities provided for the sick, there is still need of better provision in this country for convalescents, who are sent from the hospitals too weak to resume work, and still needing rest, good food, and pure air to effect a complete cure.

Two classes of invalids remain to be mentioned in this condensed summary. First, accident cases, in which the visitor must be careful to see that legal redress is obtained when the case is one for damages, and must, at the same time, protect the victim from lawyers who are glad to take a sure case for "half the proceeds." Second, incurables, for whom homes are provided requiring an entrance fee, or for whom, more often, nothing remains but the almshouse. The visitor can sometimes secure the coöperation of friends and charities interested, and so raise enough money to provide the fee for such an invalid, when, without coöperation, as much money and more would be spent and the patient remain in the end unprovided for. Charitable people often get tired; they will do a great deal for a while, and will then get interested elsewhere, and grudge the help that is still needed. In view of this failing, it is much better, in making plans for incurables, to secure a lump sum that will make adequate provision, than to depend upon the continued interest of a number of people.

The migration of invalids is the last point upon which I shall attempt to touch under this head. Any one who has visited California, Florida, Colorado, or any other part of our country where climatic conditions are supposed to be favorable for invalids, will realize the irresponsible way in which charitable people are accustomed to send the sick where they do not belong. The worst of it is that the sudden change of climate and the impossibility of securing proper care, so far from effecting a cure, in many cases hasten death. "The saddest thing about the life of a Denver minister," writes Rev. Samuel A. Eliot, "is the number of lonely funerals that he is called upon to attend. Often I have been hastily summoned to say a prayer over some poor body at the undertaker's shop, where there would be present just the undertaker and the minister, with perhaps the keeper of the boarding-house where the lad died or an officer of the Charity Organization Society. I look at the youthful victim of ignorant good-will borne to his neglected grave, I imagine the mother and sisters in the farmhouse on the New England hillside, whose tenderness might have soothed his last hours, and I think with bitterness of the well-meant but misdirected charity which condemned him to a miserable exile and a forlorn death." [1]

It must be remembered that change of climate is helpful only in the earlier stages of disease, and only then when the patient is able to live in comparative comfort, free from worry and anxiety. To send invalids to a strange place in the name of charity, without providing them with the means of subsistence, is the refinement of cruelty.

Collateral Readings: Publications of local Board of Health. Proceedings of International Congress of Charities, Chicago, 1893, volume on "Hospitals, Dispensaries,

[1] Proceedings of the Nineteenth Conference of Charities, Denver, 1892, pp. 91 *sq*.

and Nursing." "Instructive District Nursing," M. K. Sedgewick in "Forum," Vol. XXII, pp. 297 *sq*. "The Feeble-minded," Dr. George H. Knight in Proceedings of Twenty-second National Conference of Charities, pp. 150 *sq*. See also discussion in same volume, pp. 460 *sq*. " The Care of Epileptics," William P. Letchworth in Proceedings of Twenty-third National Conference of Charities, pp. 199 *sq*. "Industrial Education of Epileptics," Dr. William P. Spratling in Proceedings of Twenty-fourth National Conference of Charities, pp. 69 *sq*. " Destitute Convalescents : After Care of the Insane," Dr. Richard Dewey in the same, pp. 76 *sq*. See also discussion on pp. 464 *sq*.

CHAPTER VII

SPENDING AND SAVING

THERE is a new school of philanthropists that are inclined to make light of thrift, and to class both industry and thrift among the merely "economic virtues." To this school must belong the settlement worker who spoke of thrift as "ordinarily rather demoralizing."[1] But another objection to thrift which has been made by settlement workers is that it was only good for the working classes "until their employers discovered that there was a margin to their employees' wages."

Is it true that industry and thrift are merely economic virtues? We instinctively feel that they are something more. One has only to think of a lazy man to get an impression of something essentially contemptible and cow-

[1] See Report on the Questions drawn up by Present Residents in our College Settlements, p. 17. Published by the Church Social Union, Boston.

ardly. On the other hand the man that loves work and throws himself into it with energy is winning more than material rewards. The thriftless and the extravagant, whether rich or poor, are often mean and self-indulgent, lacking the first quality of the unselfish in lacking self-control. In teaching industry and thrift, therefore, — though these virtues, like others, have an unlovely side, — we may feel that we are dealing with two of the elements out of which not only character but all the social virtues are built.

Nor will the pessimistic theory that the worker must spend as much as possible on indifferent food and housing in order to keep up the rate of wages, bear the light of common sense. It is true that the man who merely hoards for the sake of hoarding, developing no new and higher wants, no clearly defined aims, will still be almost as helpless as the most thriftless. But no one is more helpless against the encroachments of employers than the man who lives from hand to mouth, whose necessities press ever hard upon him, crippling him and crippling those with whom he competes in the open market. Then again, successful coöperation is impossible to the thriftless. The lack of self-control, the lack of power to defer their pleasures, unfits them for combined effort and makes it more difficult for them to be loyal to their fellow-workmen. Visitors can advocate thrift, therefore, for both economic and moral reasons.

There is a use of the word "thrift" that may help us to realize its best meaning. Gardeners call a plant of vigorous growth a "thrifty" plant. Let us bear this in mind in our charitable work, and remember that anything that hinders vigorous growth is essentially unthrifty. Thrift means something more than the hoarding of small savings. In fact, saving at the expense of health, or training, or some other necessary preparation for successful living, is always unthrifty. It is unthrifty to live in damp rooms to secure cheaper rent; it is unthrifty to put aside money for burial insurance when the children are underfed; it is unthrifty either to buy patent medicines or to neglect early symptoms of disease in order to save a doctor's bill; above all, it is unthrifty to take young children away from school and force them to become breadwinners. Thrift, therefore, includes spending as well as saving.

Charity workers often complain that, in the poor families known to them, thrift is impossible, because there is nothing to save. More often than not this means that their relations with the poor have ceased as soon as acute distress is past, and that they have stopped visiting at the very time when improved material conditions have made the best friendly services possible.

Any attempt to divide the poor into classes is to be deprecated, because human beings are not easily classified. But, speaking roughly, and using the classification merely as a temporary convenience, charity workers will find that the thrift habit divides the poor into three classes. First, those who are very thrifty, and this is a large class. Misfortune may overtake the most provident during long periods of industrial depression, or they may become temporarily dependent through sickness or some unforeseen accident. The second class includes those who are willing to work when work is plentiful, but who have little persistence or resourcefulness in procuring work. In the busy season they spend lavishly on cheap pleasures and soon become applicants for relief in troubled times. Debt has no terrors for them, and, from their point of view, it is useless to save because they cannot save enough to make it seem worth while. In the third class we find the lazy and vicious, who shirk work, and, living by their wits, are better off in bad times than in good. "It is with the second class that the charitable may work lasting harm or lasting good. To let them feel that no responsibility rests with them during the busy season, and that all the responsibility rests with us to relieve their needs when the busy season is over, rapidly pushes them into the third class. To teach them, on the other hand, the power and cumulative value of the saving habit, and so get them beforehand with the world, is to place them in the first class and soon render them independent of our material help." [1]

[1] Leaflet on "Summer Savings," published by the Baltimore Charity Organization Society.

A characteristic of the second class is the habit of buying on credit. The book at the corner grocery not only tempts the purchaser into buying unnecessary things, but the prices are higher than the market rate for inferior goods. A student in a university laboratory, who is also a friendly visitor, had occasion to use some sugar in one of his experiments, and, being hurried, purchased it from the nearest corner grocery, paying more than the usual price. It proved to be badly adulterated, and the user has been more careful since in advising his poor friends about purchasing provisions. The credit system is the natural outcome of uncertain income, and for that reason is hard to avoid, but in a number of instances it is continued long after the necessity that caused the buyer to ask credit has ceased to exist.

Another and less excusable form of the credit system is buying household goods on the instalment plan. The poor are often teased into this by glib agents. An old woman, whose income was not sufficient to keep her alive, contracted to buy a clock on the instalment plan for $8.00 because she needed one when she occasionally had a day's job of cleaning. When her visitor remonstrated that a dollar clock would have done quite as well, she replied triumphantly, "Yes, but this one is only 25 cents a week!" When payments cannot be made, and the purchaser is threatened with the loss of the goods, it is possible to be too hasty in rushing to the rescue. The Fifteenth Report of the Boston Associated Charities records such an experience. "A family had purchased furniture upon the instalment plan, when the husband was suddenly deprived of his job. The furniture was about to be seized, when generous sympathizers came to the rescue, and redeemed the articles. Scarcely had the donors time to realize what a financial relief they had been able to give to the troubled family before the same bit of folly was repeated, and 'parlor furniture' was added to the inventory of goods and chattels to be paid for by the week."[1] When instalment men threaten seizure, it is well to find out whether they are acting within the law. They have been known to take advantage of ignorant clients. But the system

[1] p. 25.

itself is bad in that it encourages the purchase of unnecessary things, and at a great advance upon cash prices.

When the poor man would borrow, he is often exposed to the impositions of a class of unscrupulous money lenders, who violate the laws against usury, but hope to escape punishment or loss through the ignorance of their customers. The pitiful part of it is that the self-respecting poor often fall into their traps. A family in pecuniary straits for the first time is naturally attracted by the specious advertisements of the chattel-mortgage companies, which offer to lend money on goods that the borrower keeps in his possession, and promise that all negotiations shall be strictly confidential. This seems an easy way out of present difficulties without loss of self-respect or any painful publicity. But the terms of the contract are far from easy in reality. Through a system of bonuses, extra fees, or monthly payments for "guaranteeing" the loan, interest amounting to from 100 per cent to 200 per cent a year is wrung from the borrowers. Bled dry at last, and unable to pay such extortionate interest and the principal too, their goods are seized, and the members of the household become objects of charity. Whereever these chattel-mortgage companies gain any foothold, many of their victims are applicants for relief. The law usually furnishes ample protection, but the companies flourish through the poor man's ignorance of the law.

As soon as a visitor learns that the goods of a poor family are mortgaged, he should, at once, whether the company is pressing for payment or not, learn the terms of the contract, and get an opinion as to its validity from some friend who is a lawyer. The usual form of contract in Maryland is a six months' mortgage, bearing 6 per cent interest, with the legal charge for recording deducted from the amount advanced to the borrower. But, in addition to this, notes for from $2.00 upward, according to the size of the loan, are made payable monthly to some third party who is supposed to guarantee the loan. Lawyers advise no payments on these notes, and that principal and legal interest be offered at the expiration of the mortgage. If this offer is refused, the company renders itself liable to damage proceedings in seizing the furniture. In each case, however, it is better to have a lawyer's advice, as the contracts vary, and ignorant men, who thought they were signing a six months' mortgage, have been known to sign a one month's mortgage instead.

The law against usury can protect those who know enough to apply it, but the poor man remains unprovided with any satisfactory means of negotiating a loan. The legal rate of interest is too low to make loans on chattels profitable. The organization, by public-spirited business men, of companies that will be careful in taking risks, and will secure special legislation enabling them to charge not more than a reasonable rate of interest, is the only remedy. Companies like these have been organized successfully in Boston and Buffalo by philanthropists who were also business men and wise enough to realize the importance of placing such loan agencies on an equitable business basis. Several advantages are apparent from the working of these equitable loan companies. Those who cannot properly negotiate a loan are discouraged from applying, because the loans are made with great care. Those who get the loans are fairly dealt with, and are helped at the right time in a way that saves them from becoming applicants for charity. Best of all, the other loan companies are forced to reduce their rate of interest, and offer fairer terms.

The habit of pawning goods has never become general among our native population, but among the foreign poor of our large cities it is the common practice; and here, too, the philanthropic pawnshop, started at the instance of the New York Charity Organization Society, has reduced the percentage charged by other pawnshops in New York.

This new interest taken by philanthropy in the poor man as borrower is still in the tentative and experimental stage, but there is an encouraging analogy between its beginnings and the early history of the savings banks. "It is seldom remembered," says Mrs. Lowell, "that the great scheme of savings banks was originally conceived and put into operation as a means of helping the poor. The two first

SPENDING AND SAVING

savings banks were started in Hamburg in 1778, and in Berne in 1787, and both were more or less closely restricted to the use of domestic servants, handicraftsmen and the like. The Hamburg bank was part of the general administration of the poor funds."[1]

When the poor man attempts to save, what inducements have greatest weight with him? First of all, he is likely to save for some definite and immediate object, because he cannot spend in any effective way until he has saved. In teaching shiftless families to put by small sums, therefore, it is well to keep some definite object in view. For instance, persuade the children to save to buy needed clothing, or the parents to save to buy proper clothing, bedding, etc., for the children. This strengthens family affection and leads the way to a bank account later, by showing what money can do.[2]

Next to such immediate inducements to thrift comes the dread of pauper burial, which is a far more influential motive with the poor than the dread of either dependence or privation.

---

[1] "Public Relief and Private Charity," p. 109.
[2] See Fourth Report of Boston Associated Charities, p. 38.

Respectability is measured in poor neighborhoods by funerals, and, whether the neighborhood standards of morality and respectability are ours or not, we cannot afford, in our charity work, to ignore them. Extravagant funerals are an evil, and we should use our influence to discourage extravagance, even where it is rooted quite as much in affection as in vanity; but an unsympathetic attitude on the part of the charitable, an inability to understand the neighborhood point of view, has helped to encourage an extravagant form of saving, namely, burial and child insurance.

To enter into a discussion of the merits of industrial insurance, as furnished in this country to the poor, is outside the scope of this book, and the matter is treated quite fully, moreover, in another volume of this series ("The Development of Thrift," by Mary Willcox Brown), but the most enthusiastic advocates of industrial insurance can hardly claim for it that it is an inexpensive form of saving. A very large percentage of industrial policies lapse, and it is a common thing to find that those who have kept up their payments and have become beneficiaries, spend everything on the funeral of the insured. "Of $200.00 insurance received by one widow, $180.00 was given to the undertaker, and the remaining $20.00 was expended for a mourning outfit for herself. The family were being aided by the Emergency Society at that time."[1] In New York, the agents of the Charity Organization Society regard the following as a typical instance: A woman's husband was insured for $136.00. When he died, she called the same undertaker that had buried a child for them. His charges on the former occasion had been moderate. The woman told him that she wanted a very inexpensive funeral with only one carriage. This was the only instruction that she gave. The undertaker asked whether the deceased was insured, and was told that he was, whereupon he offered to collect the insurance and to pay over to the widow what was left. His bill amounted to $102.50. These instances do not indicate any collusion, of course, between the undertakers and the insurance companies.

[1] Eighteenth Report of Boston Associated Charities, p. 27.

We have seen in another chapter that sickness is one of the most persistent causes of distress, and only in rare instances does a death occur that has not been preceded by weeks and often months of sickness. The poor man needs sick benefits more than burial or life insurance, and the children of the poor stand in need of many other things besides decent burial. In fact, the money spent in child insurance, which can be of no possible benefit to the child, is often needed to protect the child's health or provide for its education. These should be a parent's first care from no sordid motive, and yet it is a legitimate view to regard children as an investment. The poor man has a right to expect support from his children when he is no longer able to work, and to neglect their best interests is to cripple his own future.

The beneficial societies and fraternal orders furnish a means of saving for sick benefits, but they are of such varying degrees of merit and trustworthiness that it is impossible to recommend them without qualification. They have not gained the same position that the friendly societies hold in England, partly, perhaps, because they are not subject in America to the same legal restrictions and official inspection.

Though the savings banks are open to the objection that money is too easily withdrawn from them, and is not, therefore, always available at the time of greatest need, yet, after making every allowance for this, the savings banks remain one of the safest and best means of putting by small savings. Another way of saving, which is not open to the objection of too easy withdrawals, is the purchase of shares in a good building and loan association.

Some banks provide facilities for small savings by selling special stamps of small denominations, and, in several cities, charities have established stamp saving societies to promote the saving habit, especially among children. When $5.00 has been saved in this way, a bank account should be opened. One visitor has found that, in getting children to save, it helps to have a stamp-saving card of one's own, and show it. As a means of teaching children to save, visitors should encourage the introduction of stamp savings into our public schools.

Another way to promote small savings is to send volunteer collectors among the poor, who will visit certain families weekly, and collect the five and ten cent pieces until enough has been saved to open a bank account. This work may be combined with friendly visiting, though the collector must visit at regular intervals, and in many cases it is better for the friendly visitor to visit at irregular intervals. One visitor always leaves a small bank with her family when she goes away in summer, and the unlocking of this on her return has become a family ceremony.

Saving for fuel becomes an admirable object lesson, when it is used to establish the saving habit and not allowed to stop with the mere purchase. During the summer, families can be encouraged to put by small sums weekly, and, instead of buying coal in small quantities at very high prices during the winter, can save more than half the cost by buying a ton or more early in the season.

In teaching thrift in a careless and shiftless

home, we can get many valuable suggestions from more thrifty families in the same neighborhood, or with the same income. To effectively advise about expenditure, one must know the family budget of receipts and expenditures, and often this is more than the family knows. Learning to take note of the items is the first lesson in thrift. The most important thing, however, is our own attitude of mind. "We must not get into the habit of saying, 'Poor things; they can do nothing.' We should rid ourselves of the habit of treating them, not as men and women, people who can look after themselves with strength in their muscles and brain-power in their heads, but as animals whom we allow to live in society along with ourselves, taking for granted that they are deprived of, or cannot exert, those faculties which go to make up the strength and fibre of men and women. I assure you, those who are inclined to take a sentimental turn have great temptations put before them to treat the poor as if they were dependent animals." [1]

[1] C. S. Loch in Fifteenth Report of Baltimore Charity Organization Society.

Collateral Readings: "The Development of Thrift," Miss Mary Willcox Brown. "The Standard of Life," Mrs. Bernard Bosanquet, especially the essay on "The Burden of Small Debts." Annual Reports of the Workingmen's Loan Association, Boston; the Provident Loan Association, New York; and the Provident Loan Company, Buffalo. For stamp savings, see reports of New York Charity Organization Society (Committee on Penny Provident Fund).

CHAPTER VIII

RECREATION

I HAVE said that the power to defer our pleasures is a mark of civilization. There is another mark which, in this busy America of ours, is often denied to the well-to-do as much as to the poor, and that is the power to enjoy our pleasures after we have earned them. Charity workers still underestimate the value of the power to enjoy. They are likely to regard mere contentment as a model virtue in the poor, whereas that discontent which has its root in more varied and higher wants is a splendid spur to progress. Professor F. G. Peabody quotes Lasalle in naming as one of the greatest obstructions to progress among the poor, "The cursed habit of not wanting anything." The power of enjoyment seems dead in many a down-trodden, sordid life, while in many others it wastes itself upon unworthy and degrading pleasures.

There is a passage in one of Miss Octavia Hill's essays that throws a flood of light on this question. She says that the love of adventure, the restlessness so characteristic of the Anglo-Saxon, makes him, under certain conditions, the greatest of explorers and colonizers, and that this same energy, under other conditions, helps to brutalize him. Dissatisfied with the dull round of duties that poverty enforces upon him, he seeks artificial excitement in the saloon and the gambling den. It is useless to preach contentment to such a man. We must substitute healthier excitements, other and better wants, or society will fail to reform him. In all the forms of play, all the amusements of the people, though some of them may seem to us coarse and degrading, there is this same restless seeking to express what is highest and best in man; not only to express his love of adventure, but his love of social intercourse and his love of beauty. When we once realize that certain vices are merely a perversion of good instincts, we have taken the first step toward finding their cure.

It has been said that a man's pleasures give us his true measure, and that to change the measure is to change the man. From this point of view, the subject of recreation is very near the heart of the friendly visitor's relation with the poor. We may have made a conscientious study of the family expenses and income, of the sanitary surroundings, of the work record and diet, but we shall not know the family until we know what gives them pleasure. One visitor says that she never feels acquainted with a poor family until she has had a good laugh with them. A defective sense of humor in the visitor is a great hindrance to successful work: poor people are no fonder of dismal folk than the rest of us. When we come to recreations, friendly visiting not only makes large demands upon what we know, but upon what we are. Our pleasures measure us quite as much as they measure our poor friends, and, unless we have kept fresh our own power of enjoyment, we cannot hope to impart this power to the poor, or to give them new and better wants.

Granting that we have them ourselves, what

K

are some of the healthy wants that we should try to pass on to the poor? Taking the simplest first, we should try to introduce simple games and a love of pure fun into the family circle. I am indebted to Miss Beale of the Boston Children's Aid Society for the following list of simple games, so arranged as to include standing and sitting games for each evening:

FIRST EVENING.
1. Hiding the thimble.
2. Bean bag.
3. Dominoes.

SECOND EVENING.
1. Stage coach.
2. Buzz.
3. Elements.

THIRD EVENING.
1. Hot butter blue beans.
2. Jack straws.
3. Fruit basket.

FOURTH EVENING.
1. How, when, and where.
2. Counting buzz.
3. Magical spelling.

FIFTH EVENING.
1. Go-bang.
2. Spot on the carpet.
3. Throwing lights.

SIXTH EVENING.
1. Tea-kettle.
2. Musical chairs.
3. Logomachy.

SEVENTH EVENING.
1. Telling a story.
2. Blowing the feather.
3. Authors.

EIGHTH EVENING.
1. Pigs in clover.
2. I have a rooster to sell.
3. Courtesying.

In teaching such games it is best to begin with the children, but the parents can sometimes be induced to join in. Story-telling is also an unfailing resource in our efforts to amuse the children.

But, during a good part of the year, there are many outdoor games in which the children can be interested, and, now that the trolley cars have brought the country so much nearer, country trips for the whole family should be planned at frequent intervals. There are few things more pathetic than the dread with which many of our city poor think of the country, and to teach them country pleasures is to restore to them a birthright of which they have been robbed. A love of plants and window-gardening is another healthful pleasure. Mignonette, geranium, wandering Jew, and saxifrage grow well in small spaces. To one family, living in tenement rooms where there was no sun, a visitor gave a pot of geranium. Later, the woman said: "We have taken it out on the roof every day when it was pleasant to let the sun shine on it. When I couldn't take it, Mary did; and, for fear it should get stolen, we stay and sit by it. I take the baby with me too, and the baby likes the sun as well as the flower does."

With all the added interest in outdoor exercise, and the freer, healthier life of our time, we are slow to pass such advantages on to the poor. The women of the family need much urging, sometimes, to get them to take any outdoor exercise. Bicycles are becoming cheaper, and a bicycle would be a good investment in any family where all the adults are working at indoor occupations. If the visitor find a gymnasium not too far away, the boys and their father should be induced to go to it. With these added interests, a holiday will no longer be a thing to be dreaded by the wife and mother, for there will be interesting things to do, instead of mere loafing on the corner or at the saloon. One visitor helped to cure a man of drinking by getting him an accordion — a fact that has a touch of pathos, as indicating the poverty of interests in the poor fellow's life.

The pleasures of books, music, and pictures ought to touch every life at some point. Some æsthetic pleasures, it is true, are won only after long study and preparation, but the best art is universal in its appeal. So far as books are concerned, our free libraries have made us familiar with this view. The visitor should know the rules of the nearest library, and should be ready to go there with some member of the family, in case it is unknown to them. The saloon-keepers in Ward 10, Boston, complain that the new branch of the Public Library opened there has interfered with their business. Beside encouraging the use of a lending library, the visitor should be ready to lend books, newspapers, and magazines, and should be glad to borrow a book from the family, when this will help to strengthen friendly relations.

The refining influence of good pictures is just beginning to be recognized by the charitable. Friendly visitors cannot always organize large loan exhibitions, such as are given in the poorer neighborhoods of London, New York, and Boston, but they can lend a good photograph or engraving, when they are going away, and can replace it, from time to time, by another picture. Such loans have been known, like the Eastlake screen in Stockton's story, to revolutionize the arrangement of the household. Then, too, a picture often conveys a lesson more effectively than a sermon can. Mrs. Barnett tells, in "Practicable Socialism,"[1] of a loan exhibition in Whitechapel, where Oxford students acted as guides and explained the pictures. "Mr. Schmalz's picture of 'Forever' had one evening been beautifully explained, the room being crowded by some of the humblest people, who received the explanation with interest, but in silence. The picture represented a dying girl to whom her lover had been playing his lute, until, dropping it, he seemed to be telling her with impassioned words that his love is stronger than death, and that, in spite of the grave and separation, he will love her *forever*. I was standing outside the exhibition in the half-darkness, when two girls, hatless, with one shawl between them thrown round both their shoulders, came out. They might not be living the worst life, but, if not, they were low down enough to be familiar with it, and to see

[1] pp. 119 *sq*.

in it only the relation between men and women. The idea of love lasting beyond this life, making eternity real, a spiritual bond between man and woman, had not occurred to them until the picture with the simple story was shown them. 'Real beautiful, ain't it all?' said one. 'Ay, fine, but that "Forever" I did take on with that,' was the answer."

I have lived nearly all my life in a community where, during the last twenty-five years, there has been a great change in musical taste. George Peabody left money to found a Conservatory of Music, and a few music lovers spent time and money to keep alive an Oratorio Society. Later, the visits of Thomas' Orchestra and of the Boston Symphony Orchestra added to the strength of these local musical centres; but for many years the Peabody Conservatory was ridiculed and misunderstood, and the Oratorio Society was usually in financial straits. I mention these facts, because persons who are dependent upon the Conservatory and the visiting orchestras for all the good music they know have said to me that it must be impossible for poor people ever to appreciate good music. But for the benefactions of George Peabody, and of Mr. Higginson (who made the Boston Orchestra possible), and of a few others, they themselves could never have known the pleasure of enjoying great and noble music, and, to this extent, at least, they are as dependent as the poorest; but they are quite sure that the great composers have no message for the poor. There is difficult music, of course, which only the scholarly musician can appreciate; but much of the very best music, if we once have a chance to become familiar with it, appeals to all of us. Then the artistic temperament is not a matter of either condition or race, as one of our young American musicians has pointed out. Lecturing with musical illustrations to audiences on the East Side in New York, and to audiences of negroes in Philadelphia, he is convinced that "if good music were accessible to the masses, it would be appreciated, and go far to elevate them."

"My boy," wailed a poor mother, "was that fond of music it took him straight to the bad!" And no wonder, for music — apart from the tawdriest of gospel hymn tunes — meant for him the saloon and the low concert hall. We need, to counteract such influences, plenty of cheap concerts of good music; concerts following the plan of Theodore Thomas with his well-to-do audiences, who were given first the best that they liked, and then were taught gradually to like better and better selections.

All the higher recreations encroach upon the field of education, and I am tempted to mention, in passing, some of the most promising educational efforts for encouraging study among the people. The American Society for the Extension of University Teaching, which has its headquarters at Philadelphia, has conducted very successful courses of lectures in poor neighborhoods. The enormous attendance upon the free evening lectures given by the Department of Education in New York school buildings is also significant. The popularity of the educational classes in working girls' clubs, Christian associations, and people's institutes is another good sign. But I mention these here merely to emphasize their importance as tools for the visitor. In families where an ambition has been aroused, the visitor should foster it by making connection with some such educational agencies.

There is a very obvious form of snobbery that we are quick enough to detect, the snobbery that looks down on people who have to work hard and wear shabby clothes. But an even more dangerous form of snobbery, because not so obvious, is the intellectual form, which claims an exclusive right to culture, and looks down upon the simple and unsophisticated. The fact is, that, save for a very gifted few, we are all of us dependent upon the gifts of others for what we know and what we enjoy. Probably there never was a neighborhood so exclusive but many were there upon whom education, refinements, and beautiful things were quite wasted; and there never was a neighborhood so poor but some were there who longed for beauty, education, and a larger and fuller life.

It will be seen in the next chapter that, when we attempt to supply the poor with the necessities of life, our path is beset with difficulties. But when we give them those things which, though not necessary to life, yet refine and elevate it, we can do them only unmixed good. Gifts of books, flowers, growing plants, pictures, and simple decorations, or, as in one instance known to me, the present of several rolls of light-colored wall-paper to brighten a dark room — these help to express our friendliness, and have an added value as coming from a friend. Above all, however, we should not hesitate to share with the poor our delight in healthful and refining pleasures, and should find it natural to talk freely with them about our own interests.

Collateral Readings: "Parlor Games for the Wise and Otherwise," H. E. H. "Faggots for the Fireside," Mrs. L. P. Hale. "American Girls' Own Book of Work and Play," Mrs. Helen Campbell. "Gymnastic Games," published by Boston Normal School of Gymnastics. "Methods of Social Reform," W. S. Jevons. "Picture Exhibitions in Lower New York," A. C. Bernheimer in "Forum," Vol. XIX, pp. 610 *sq*.

CHAPTER IX

RELIEF

I HAVE been very unfortunate if, in the foregoing chapters, I have failed to make it clear that there are many ways of assisting the poor in their homes besides the one way usually implied by the word "assistance." To one who knows the real needs of the poor, the relief of suffering by gifts of food and fuel seems only a small part of the work of charity; but the fact remains that the majority of mankind are still little moved by any needs that are not closely associated with hunger and cold. Their imaginations are sluggish, and the whole problem of poverty appears to them simpler than it really is. It seems to them no more than a sum in arithmetic, — "one beggar, one loaf; ten thousand beggars, ten thousand loaves"; and the charitable loaf is supposed to have moral and healing qualities that are denied to other loaves. The truth is that charitable cash and commodities have no moral qualities in themselves; not even the good intentions of the giver can endow them with peculiar virtues. Like all other commodities, however, they may become agents of either good or evil. The way in which we handle commodities tests us at every turn; tests our sincerity, our honor, our sense of spiritual things. Material relief tests us too. If we give it believing that, in itself, it can carry any blessing to the poor, we are taking a grossly material view of human life. If, on the other hand, our knowledge of the mischief done by reckless giving makes us morbidly sceptical of all material assistance, we are losing a valuable tool; for relief at the right time, and given in the right way, may be made an incentive to renewed exertion, and a help to a higher standard of living.

When the visitor's ingenuity in developing resources within the family renders material relief from outside unnecessary, the family is fortunate; but often relief from outside is a necessity, and the question then arises, How shall it be given? Everything depends upon the "how."

First of all — and this is a lesson that visitors are slow to learn — it is very unwise, especially in the first months of acquaintance, for friendly visitors to give money or commodities to the families they visit, though they may find it necessary to see that relief is sent from some other source. "If one of our visitors finds her family in dire distress, and there is no time to go to the office and have aid secured in some other way, she of course, like any one else, furnishes it at once from her own pocket. But except in these rare emergencies, our visitors do not themselves give relief to those they visit. We believe this is a wise rule, and after eight years' experience we would not change it. If a stranger offered you a gift, you would feel insulted and refuse it. Suppose you were constrained by necessity to accept it — would it not make a certain bar between you and that stranger very difficult to break down? Imagine yourself of a different temper, that you wanted all you could get. Would you not be likely to talk more freely or truthfully to one who you knew would give you nothing than to one from whom you hoped a plausible tale would draw a dollar? For the visitor's sake also the rule is a good one. We are apt to think our duty done if we have given money, and if we cannot do that, we are forced to use our ingenuity to find other and better ways of helping."[1]

It is eleven years since the foregoing passage was written, but the experience of almost every practical worker in charity will confirm it. Friendly visitors are human, and their task, as it has been described in this book, is not an easy one. It is so much easier to give. But the history of many volunteers in charity is that, starting out with excellent intentions, they were tempted to give relief to the families they visited. First it was clothing for the children, then the rent, then groceries, then more clothing, and the family's needs, strange to say, seemed to increase, until, finding their suggestions unheeded, and

[1] Miss Z. D. Smith in Report of Union Relief Association of Springfield, Mass., 1887, p. 12.

the people no better off, the volunteers deserted their post, and, still worse, carried away a false, distorted idea of what poor people are like. The poor, too, learn to distrust a charitable interest that is not continuous. A little self-restraint, a little more determination to keep their purpose clearly in mind, would save the charitable and the poor from an experience that is hardening to both.

When the friendly visitor has known a family for years, and the friendship is thoroughly established, it is conceivable that he may be the best possible source of relief; but the attitude that we must guard against — creeping, as it does, into all our relations with the poor as an inheritance, an outworn tradition — is the attitude of the London church visitor, who said that she could not possibly administer spiritual consolation without a grocery ticket in her bag. It is good for the poor and good for us to learn that other and more natural relations are possible than the relations of giver and receiver, of patron and patronized.

Nothing that has been said, however, against

permitting the visitor to become the source of supplies should be interpreted as meaning that the visitor is not to concern himself with the way in which relief enters the home, and its effect upon the welfare of the family. Everything that concerns the welfare of its members concerns him, and that their energies should be paralyzed by a too plentiful supply of relief, or that the lack of it should cause unnecessary suffering, is a matter that concerns him vitally. To administer relief wisely one needs special training, and an inexperienced visitor should seek the advice of one who knows the charitable resources of his own particular community and the standard of living of the family's particular neighborhood. There are certain general relief principles that common sense and experience have found to be applicable everywhere, however, and, avoiding the technical language of charitable experts, I shall try to state these principles as briefly and clearly as possible, under six heads.

I. When relief is needed in a poor home, it should be given *in the home* without any publicity, and after conference with the head of the family, who, if unable to provide the means of subsistence himself, is still responsible for procuring it. The man of the family, unless disabled, should do all the asking. This means, of course, that wives should not be sent to charity offices and private families to ask assistance, and that every charitable agency, public and private, and every church worker and every teacher should positively refuse to receive any message or appeal for relief sent by a child, except in those rare cases where all the adult members of the family are disabled. The neglect of this simple precaution has often kept children away from school, and has tempted parents to use them to excite sympathy. One sensational item in a Baltimore daily, headed "Barefooted through the Snow," was the account of thinly clad children sent to the police station for relief. Their father, upon investigation, was found to have taken their shoes off, and sent them out to do the begging for the family, after refusing a good offer of work.

This newspaper item illustrates the danger of giving publicity to individual cases of need. The poor read the papers, and when they find that sympathy is excited by sending children for relief, they are tempted to use their children in the same way. Few worse things can happen to a poor family than for their distress to excite the interest of an enterprising journalist, who publishes an account of the circumstances with name and address. It brings them an avalanche of relief sometimes, but the visits from sentimental strangers, the envy of their worst neighbors and the disapproval of their best, the excitement and uncertainty, the repeating over and over the tale of their trouble, and the destruction of all the natural conditions of family life, leave behind a train of demoralization that lasts long after the relief has been exhausted.

In a less degree, the congregating of the poor in any place for a relief distribution is to be deplored, whether the relief is given out upon presentation of an order or not. The standing in line, the jostling and waiting, the gregariousness and publicity, are demoralizing.

Missions, I regret to say, sometimes treat such free distributions as an advertising spectacle; but "it is of the very essence of charity that it should be private," and advertising, on the other hand, presupposes publicity. I have often had opportunities to give the poor tickets for Christmas dinners, free treats, and general charitable distributions, but, as I have come to know the poor better, and to care more for their welfare, I have learned to resent a charity that would help them in droves, as if they were cattle. A form of charitable relief that appeals to many good people in cold weather is the free-soup kitchen, where the poor come with their kettles, and "no questions are asked." The hot, steaming soup and the cold, shivering applicants make a striking contrast, and the kind-hearted citizen is very likely to think of such charity as "practical," and denounce the people who object to it as "theorists." There is nothing practical about a free-soup kitchen. It is the cheapest of cheap charity. If the weather is cold, people must have fires at home to keep them from freezing, and the gift of cooked food is unnecessary. Soup is not the most nourishing food to give, moreover, and the "no questions asked" means that those who need most will get least, and that the crowd of sturdy beggars always attracted by such distributions will drive away the shrinking poor, who need help the most.

The first relief principle is that relief should be given individually and privately in the home, and that the head of the family should be conferred with on all questions of relief.

II. A due regard for the self-respect of the poor prompts us, when relief is needed, to secure it from the most natural source or sources. A family that still has credit does not need relief at all, and it is better for them to run in debt to those who still consider them a fair business risk than to receive charity instead. Next to credit, as a natural resource, come relatives. Charity weakens natural ties by stepping in, unless it is certain that relatives have done all that they can, or unless it has brought pressure to bear, at least, to induce them to do their part. Sometimes relatives have good reasons, which the charitable should know and heed, for withholding relief. The next source of relief is friends, including neighbors and former employers, and a visitor who is seeking aid for a family may often discover better ways of helping by consulting with these. The tendency of indiscriminate charity is to destroy neighborliness. (See p. 27.) The next source is the church to which members of the family belong, or fraternal societies of which they may have been members. Only when all these sources fail, and it is not possible to get adequate relief from charitable individuals whom we can interest, should we turn to societies organized for the purpose of giving relief to the poor, and, even then, special societies, like the St. Andrew's Society for Scots, St. George's Society for Englishmen, and Hebrew Benevolent Society for Hebrews, should take precedence of general relief societies, which were not intended to assume other people's charitable burdens, but exist to care for the unbefriended families that cannot be relieved from any more natural source.

There remains one more source of relief for the poor in their own homes. Many American cities still give public outdoor relief. This relief is called "public" because it is voted from funds collected by taxation, and it is called "outdoor" to distinguish it from indoor or institutional relief. There are several reasons for regarding this as the least desirable form of relief. In the first place, it is often administered by politicians, and becomes a source of political corruption. But, what is even more important, it is official and therefore not easily adaptable to varying needs. Private charities can undertake a large expenditure for one family, when a large expenditure will put the family beyond the need of charity; but official relief must always be hampered by the fear of establishing a precedent, and inadequate relief is often the result of this fear. Moreover, public relief comes from what is regarded as a practically inexhaustible source, and people who once receive it are likely to regard it as a right, as a permanent pension, implying no obligation on their part. Even where it is well and honestly administered, as in Boston, the most experienced charity workers regard it as a source of demoralization both to the poor and the charitable. No public agency can supply the devoted, friendly, and intensely personal relation so necessary in charity. It can supply the gift, but it cannot supply the giver, for the giver is a compulsory tax rate. Some of the sources of information on this subject are noted at the end of the chapter. It is impossible to give the question any adequate consideration here, but it will be noticed that a large majority of those who have worked as volunteers in the homes of the poor, and have watched the effects of outdoor relief in these homes, are anxious to see it abolished in all our large cities, believing that private and voluntary charity can more than replace it. On the other hand, those who know the poor in another way — in public offices and from the point of view of the public official — are often stanch advocates of outdoor relief.

The fewer sources of relief for any one family the better, though it is often impossible to get adequate relief from one source. "The difficulty in giving judiciously is great, even where one person or society does the whole. But when the applicant goes from one to another, undergoing repeated temptations to deceive and getting from no one what is sufficient to meet the full need, each giver feeling but a partial responsibility in the matter, one giving when another has desired that relief ought to be withheld, and thus destroying the effect of the other's action, we believe that the difficulties in the way of judicious aid are greatly increased. . . . We earnestly hope that the various relief-giving agencies may adopt the plan, so far as possible, of a division of labor, each doing all the relief-giving needed by those within its care and leaving others to do the relief-giving in other cases."[1] When, however, relief must come from a number of sources, it does most good if given through one channel.

The second relief principle is that we should seek the most natural and least official sources of relief, bearing in mind the ties of kinship, friendship, and neighborliness, and that we should avoid the multiplication of sources.

III. In deciding to give or to withhold relief, we should be guided by its probable effect upon the future of the applicant. When it is con-

[1] Fifth Report of Boston Associated Charities, pp. 31 *sq*.

ceded that we should discriminate at all in giving, the popular notion is that we should give to the worthy poor, and refuse aid to the unworthy. The words "worthy" and "unworthy" mean very little; they are mere catchwords to save us from thinking. When we say that people are "worthy," we mean, I suppose, that they are worthy of material relief, but no one is so worthy as to be absolutely relief-proof. If relief is given without plan or purpose, it will injure the worthiest recipient. On the other hand, an intelligent visitor can often see his way clear to effect very great improvement in what are called "unworthy" cases, and may find material relief a necessary means to this end. Better than any hard and fast classification, is the principle that our relief should always have a future to it, should be given as part of a carefully devised plan for making the recipient permanently better off. The only excuse for giving relief without a plan is that it is sometimes necessary to give what is called "interim relief," to prevent present suffering, until we can learn all the facts and a plan can be devised. In this, relief work is very much like doctoring a sick patient. We have very little use for a doctor who does not alleviate suffering promptly, but, on the other hand, we naturally mistrust the doctor who does not ask a great many questions, or who fails to make a plan for getting his patient beyond the need of medicine as soon as possible. Our relief work is often nothing but aimless dosing. Like the doctor, too, we should stand ready to change our plan of treatment when conditions change. "In one family, where a pension was given on account of the breadwinner's illness, and continued for six weeks after his death, the daughters have been unwilling to take work offered at wages they thought too low, because they were not thrown upon their own resources at once."[1]

A plan that is not based upon the actual facts is, of course, worse than useless. Sometimes a charitable person will call at a home for the first time, will see miserable surroundings, and will feel that the circumstances are all made plain to him in one visit. Calling at a relief office, he will urge immediate relief, adding, "I have investigated the case myself."

[1] Eighth Report of Boston Associated Charities, p. 25.

The word "investigation" means very different things to different people. Here are some of the questions that, according to the London "Charity Organization Review,"[1] an almoner should ask himself about any given case:

"1. Can anything be done to increase the family income? Can the number of wage-earners be added to? Can those doing badly paid work be taught better-paid work? Can they be put in the way of getting better tools or appliances?

"2. Can anything be done to make the existing income go farther than it goes now? *e.g.*

"(*a*) Is too much money paid away in rent? Could as good accommodations be obtained in the district elsewhere for less? Or could the family do with less accommodation.

"(*b*) Is money wasted? *e.g.* on medicine, or in habitual pawning, or in purchasing from tallymen, or in buying things not wanted? Do husband and children keep back an undue share of their earnings?

"(*c*) Is too much money spent in travelling

[1] Vol. II, New Series, p. 224.

backwards and forwards to place of employment? If so, could the family move nearer to their work without increasing their rent?

"These are but a few of the questions which the almoner must put if he wishes to be thorough. In every case he must *think* about the problem with which he is dealing, and he must try to make those who are applying for help think also."

The best arguments for giving relief upon a definite plan are the results of haphazard benevolence that are all around us — feeble-minded women with illegitimate offspring, children crippled by drunken fathers, juvenile offenders who began as child-beggars, aged parents neglected by their children. Every form of human weakness and depravity is intensified by the charity that asks no questions.

The third relief principle is that relief should look not only to the alleviation of present suffering, but to promoting the future welfare of the recipient.

IV. It follows from the foregoing that when we relieve at all we should relieve adequately.

"Can any one really approve of inadequate

relief? Can any one really approve of giving 50 cents to a man who must have $5.00, trusting that some one else will give the $4.50, and knowing that, to get it, the person in distress must spend not only precious strength and time, but more precious independence and self-respect? . . .

"There are many families in every city who get relief (only a little to be sure, but enough to do harm) who ought never to have one cent, — families where the man can work, but will not work. The little given out of pity for his poor wife and children really intensifies and prolongs their suffering, and only prevents the man from doing his duty by making him believe that, if he does not take care of them, some one else will. On the other hand, there are many families who ought to have their whole support given to them for a few years, — widows, for instance, who cannot both take care of and support their children, and yet who ought not to have to give them up into the blighting care of an institution; and these families get nothing, or get so little that it does them no good at all, only serving to keep them also in misery and to raise false hopes, or else to teach them to beg to make up what they must have.

"Ought not charitable people to manage in some way to remedy these two opposite evils? — to do more for those who should have more, and to do nothing for those who should have nothing, saving money by discriminating, and thus having enough to give adequate relief in all cases." [1]

By adequate relief charity workers do not mean that all *apparent* needs should be met. There are often resources that are hidden from the inexperienced eye, and by ignoring these we destroy them.

The fourth relief principle is that, instead of trying to give a little to very many, we should help adequately those that we help at all.

V. We should make the poor our partners in any effort to improve their condition, and relief should be made dependent upon their doing what they can for themselves. Whether we give or do not give, our reasons should be

[1] Mrs. Josephine Shaw Lowell in Proceedings of Twenty-third National Conference of Charities, New Haven, 1895, p. 49.

clearly stated, and we should avoid driving any sordid bargain with them. For instance, it may be wise sometimes to make relief conditional, among other things, upon attending church, but to require attendance upon a church to which they do not belong because it is our church, or to let them regard relief as in any way associated with making converts to our way of thinking, is to weaken our influence and tempt the poor to deceive us.

The fifth relief principle is that we should help the poor to understand the right relations of things by stating clearly our reasons for giving or withholding relief, and by requiring their hearty coöperation in all efforts for their improvement.

VI. The form of relief must vary with individual circumstances and needs. Work that is real work is better, of course, than any relief; but there should be a prejudice among charity workers against sham work, for which there is no demand in the market. Unless such work is educational, or is used to test the applicant's willingness to work, it is often better to give material relief.

A charitable superstition that we should outgrow is the notion that it saves us from pauperizing the poor to call our gifts loans. We may know that they cannot repay, and they may know that we know it, but this juggling with words is still undeservedly popular. When the chances of their being able to repay are reasonably good, and a loan is made, we should be as careful to collect the debt as in any business transaction.

Another charitable superstition is the prejudice in favor of relief in kind rather than in money. We think that bundles of groceries and clothes, and small allowances of fuel, can do no harm, but the fact is that, where it would be unsafe to give money, it is usually unsafe to give money's equivalent. Large relief societies find it more economical to buy commodities in quantities, and so get the advantage of wholesale prices; but, so far as the poor themselves are concerned, there is no reason for giving goods rather than cash. On the contrary, many poor people can make the money go farther than we can. Money intended for temporary relief should not be used for rent, however, except in cases where ejectment would seriously endanger the welfare of the family. Back rent is like any other back debt; landlords should take their chances of loss with other creditors. Nor should charitable relief be used to enable people to move from place to place in order to avoid the payment of rent.[1]

When institutional care is clearly not only the most economical but the most adequate form of relief, we are sometimes justified in refusing all other forms.

In cases where institutional care is not practicable, and relief will be needed for a long period, it is best to organize a private pension, letting all the natural sources of relief combine and give through one medium an adequate amount.

The sixth relief principle is that we must find that form of relief which will best fit the particular need.

Though the foregoing six relief principles could easily be extended to twenty, yet a book-

[1] See Fifteenth Annual Report of the New York Charity Organization Society, pp. 44 *sq.*, and p. 55.

ful of such generalizations would be of no value to the almoner without a detailed knowledge of the neighborhood into which relief is to go, and an intimate acquaintance with the lives of the poor. It is evident, therefore, that a beginner in charity should not decide relief questions except in consultation with an experienced worker. For instance, a new visitor going to the house of a widow supporting her aged mother and two children, may find the woman sick, and receiving only a small pittance in sick benefits from the society to which she belongs. There is no apparent suffering, but the visitor at once concludes that the income is insufficient, and applies to the nearest relief agency, asking that coal be sent. As a matter of fact, the family income is as large as the average income of the neighborhood, and the woman has never thought of asking relief; if fuel is sent, the neighbors all know it, and, immediately, there is a certain expectancy aroused, a certain spirit of speculation takes the place of the habit of thrift. There seem, to the simple imaginations of these people, to be exhaustless stores of relief, which are somehow at the command of visiting ladies. Take another instance of a more difficult kind. A family has long passed the stage of receiving relief for the first time; the man is a heavy drinker, the household filthy, the children neglected. They appeal at once for assistance. The children need shoes to go to Sunday-school, the rent is overdue, the coal is out. Confronted with such misery, the beginner is very likely to give, and to compound with his conscience by giving "a little." This is the very treatment that has brought them to their present pass, and only an experienced and intelligent almoner can tell how far it is wise to let the forces of nature work a cure, and how far it is wise to prevent extreme suffering by interference.

One trouble in the past has been that the agents employed by relief societies have not always been intelligent, but there have been great advances made in this regard, and now, in many communities, the agents of charitable societies are active, intelligent men and women, who have received special training for the work. These agents are often in communication with many sources of relief, and can save us from duplicating relief to the same persons — from sending it, that is, where others are meeting the same need already. There are many reasons, therefore, for doing our charitable work in consultation with an experienced almoner, and friendly visiting, where it has failed, has usually failed through the visitor's unwarranted assumption that the giving of material relief was a simple and easy matter, about which charity workers made an unnecessary lot of trouble.

Collateral Readings: "The English Poor Law," Rev. T. Fowle. "The Beggars of Paris," translated from the French of M. Paulian by Lady Herschell. "Outdoor Relief," see Warner's "American Charities," pp. 162 *sq*. "Economic and Moral Effect of Outdoor Relief," Mrs. Josephine Shaw Lowell in Proceedings of Seventeenth National Conference of Charities, pp. 81 *sq*. "Outdoor Relief: Arguments for and against," in Proceedings of Eighteenth National Conference of Charities, pp. 28 *sq*. "Relief in Work," P. W. Ayres in Proceedings of Nineteenth National Conference of Charities, pp. 436 *sq*. "Is Emergency Relief by Work Wise?" the same in Proceedings of Twenty-second National Conference of Charities, pp. 96 *sq*.

CHAPTER X

THE CHURCH

Relief agents working in our great cities usually find that, in answer to direct questions, the poor are likely to claim connection with some one of the large denominations, though further acquaintance will often reveal the fact that this connection is merely nominal. There are, of course, many poor people that are active church members, but in spite of the wonderful activity of all branches of the Christian church during the last fifty years, in spite of the multiplication of missions and the devotion of many good men and women to their upbuilding, the fact remains that many of the very poor are still outside the churches. In trying to explain this, we have to take into account certain external conditions, such as the natural shrinking of the less fortunate from social contact, and the migratory habits of the poor;

but another very important factor in this alienation is, I believe, the preoccupation of the church with material relief and with those who clamor for it.

Some of the very poor are ready enough to connect themselves with the church, but, attending its services and receiving its ministrations with the one idea of getting assistance, it is not too much to say of them that they are "pious for revenue only." And yet, in saying this, it is necessary to qualify it at once by the statement that the fault rests not so much with the ignorant poor as with the multiplied and rival church agencies that tempt them to hypocrisy and deceit. If the church could only have a good, wholesome, terrifying vision, and see itself as the poor see it!

"A friend of mine," writes a London charity worker, "heard two very respectable women talking. One said, 'Well, Mrs. Smith, how have you fared this Christmas?' 'Oh, very badly; I had very little relief.' The other replied: 'Well, Mrs. Smith, it is all your own fault; you will go and sit in the side aisle of the church, where nobody ever sees you. If you would sit in front, you would be helped as we all are.'" Writing of conditions too common in America, Rev. George B. Safford says: "Families transfer their connection from one church to another, or, with an impartiality rare in other relations, distribute their representatives among several Sunday-schools or churches, gaining by pseudo-devout arts what they can from each: Methodist clothing; Baptist groceries; Presbyterian meat; Episcopalian potatoes; Roman Catholic rent; Universalist cash, available for 'sundries,'—all are acceptable to the mendicant pensioner of religious charity. One family, now at last well advertised, in an eastern city found its numerous youthful progeny effective leeches as applied to the several Sunday-schools among which they were distributed. The 'widowed' mother underwent frequent conversion; the children enjoyed the benefit of as frequent baptism. On a certain gathering of clergymen of different churches, when one after another had told the story of his discomfiture, all joined to congratulate the single representative of the Baptist denomination present on his happy escape from the imposture, under which several others had in turn baptized the children. But from him came the sad confession that he had baptized the woman herself."[1] In my own city, a family made a small child not their own a source of income by having it baptized frequently in different churches, so that three charitable members of three Episcopal churches were astonished to find, on comparing notes, that they shared the responsibility of being the child's godmothers.

But it is needless to multiply illustrations; almost every church has a collection of such experiences, and the bad effects of successful deception upon the deceivers are apparent enough. I pass to the important fact that this class of the poor, though numerically insignificant by comparison with the poor in general, are yet so much in evidence as the objects of Christian zeal, and the church wastes so much time in coddling them, that the self-respecting poor often hold aloof. It is a common thing to hear a poor man say that he is not going to attend church, and be suspected of

[1] "Charities Review," Vol. II, pp. 26 *sq*.

trying to get something. It does not increase his respect for Christians to find them easily deceived, and it outrages his sense of justice to see that laziness, drunkenness, and vice are rewarded by church workers. Even among tramps, the variety known as the "mission bum" is looked down upon by his fellows, and there is a lesson for the mission worker in this simple fact.

In writing thus frankly of home missionary work, I am not unmindful of all the difficulties with which Christian ministers have to contend. Many of them are as much alive to the dangers of indiscriminate relief as any one can be, and many of them have risked unpopularity and misunderstanding to lift their churches out of the tread-mill of ineffectual, dole-dispensing charities into vital contact with the needs of the poor. The difficulties of Christian ministers are twofold. Their first duty is to develop the charitable instincts of church members, to overcome the selfishness and inertia of the natural man. When they have succeeded in arousing a desire to do something for somebody else, they must also furnish ample opportunity for the exercise of this newly awakened impulse. Now the charitable development of the individual follows the development of the race; the individual outgrows slowly, if at all, the sentimental and patronizing view of poverty. To carry church members beyond this phase and make them effective workers, genuine powers of leadership are needed, and it is much easier to let them follow their own devices. We have seen in the last chapter that relief work, if well done, is the most difficult of all charitable work, but nine inexperienced workers out of every ten will think it the best and easiest means of helping the poor — the only means, in fact.

A difficulty to be reckoned with, and yet one with which it is hard to have any patience, is the rank materialism that regards relief as a legitimate means of attracting people to the church. Relief as a gospel agency has done far more harm than good: you cannot buy a Christian without getting a bad bargain, and yet, competition among rival churches working in the same poor neighborhood is so sharp that even now, in these days of coöperative effort, we find that the sordid appeal is made. "I call it waste," wrote the late Archbishop of Canterbury, "when money is laid out upon instinct which ought to be laid out upon principle, and waste of the worst possible kind when two or three religious bodies are working with one eye to the improvement of the condition of those whom they help, and with another eye directed to getting them within the circle of their own organization. When each of those religious bodies does so work, say upon a single large family, and, feeling quite sure of one member of the family, nourishes great hopes of the rest of the members of the family that they will become true and orthodox members of their own community, I call that not only waste — I call it demoralization of the worst conceivable kind, for a reason which the poet puts thus, 'What shall bless when holy water banes?' The demoralization produced is the worst possible, because the highest possible thoughts are used as mere instruments for low ends."[1]

[1] "Occasional Papers of the London Charity Organization Society," p. 35.

One result of using relief as a bribe is that the gift no longer has for its sole object the relief of distress, or the restoration of the receiver to independence, and is likely, therefore, to be inadequate. "One clergyman with whom I remonstrated on the uselessness of giving 1*s*. when 20*s*. was needed, said it was impossible for him to do as we did and give adequate relief, as it would cause jealousy amongst both district visitors and parishioners if he gave more to one case than to another, so 2*s*. 6*d*. was generally the limit." [1]

In enumerating the natural sources of relief, I have mentioned the church after relatives, friends, and neighbors. The church is not a natural source of relief when it becomes a general relief agency, giving inadequate doles to large numbers of dependents. It is a natural source of relief for those who have sought its ministrations from religious motives; when these become dependent, it is the church's privilege to aid them privately, ten-

[1] Miss Pickton in London "Charity Organization Review," Vol. X, p. 538.

derly, and adequately. Even beyond its own membership, the church can safely undertake the giving of material relief, when this is incidental to the carrying out of other plans for the benefit of the poor; incidental, for instance, to the work of friendly visiting, with a view to furthering a visitor's plans for improving a family's condition. But the gift must be free from the suspicion of proselytizing.

Protestants often criticise the Roman Catholic church for expecting the very poor to pay toward the support of the church. They criticise, in their ignorance, one of the wisest measures taken by the Church of Rome for strengthening its hold upon the people. Poor Roman Catholics are far more likely than poor Protestants to think of the church as belonging to them, as a power which exists not only for them but through them. Wherever the Protestant church has gained an equally strong hold upon the poor, it has made equal demands upon their loyalty and self-sacrifice.

After all has been said in objection to past

and present methods of church charity, we must realize that, if the poor are to be effectually helped by charity, the inspiration must come from the church. The church has always been and will continue to be the chief source of charitable energy; and I believe that, to an increasing degree, the church will be the leader in charitable experiment and in the extension of the scope of charitable endeavor. In the church or nowhere we must find acceptance for the methods advocated in this book. In the church or nowhere we must seek the organized devotion that shall protect the children of the poor from greed and neglect, that shall advance sanitary and educational reforms, that shall supply purer and higher amusements for the people, and shall bring to them more and more, as time goes on, of the advantages of modern life. The church has already been the pioneer in such work. In cities where kindergartens are now a part of the public school system, the first free kindergartens were supported by the churches, and large charities, now secularized, were supported by churches until they had passed the stage of experiment. Secular agencies are still dependent upon the churches for workers that can bring the right spirit to charitable work.

Instead of multiplying agencies needlessly, the city churches will find it to the advantage of their spiritual work to keep up vital connection with city charities. A clergyman who has an active church in one of our eastern cities, has abandoned the plan of starting separate church schools, societies, or institutions, realizing that many of these are unnecessary, and that many others, necessary in themselves, are inadequately supported. His people are sent instead, according to their aptitudes, to hospitals, children's charities, societies for visiting the needy, almshouses, and homes for the aged. It may be objected that the shoulder-to-shoulder contact, the strength of concentration, is lacking in such a plan. But the church holds frequent congregational meetings, where all who have been detailed to serve as friendly visitors, hospital workers, etc., report to the church and to the minister. Each one learns in this way from the work of the others; weak points in the city's plans for dealing with the poor are made apparent; and the church is able by united effort to obtain needed reforms. The work is understood to be a practical application of the gospel as taught from the church pulpit, and there is a natural and vital connection between the spiritual and social life of the church community. Two other advantages are apparent. The elasticity of the plan makes it possible to find work adapted to many varying capacities, and all denominational rivalry, all petty jealousy is avoided.

The friendly visitor from such a church will not visit the poor with a view to winning them away from other churches to his own. On the other hand, he will see the importance of some church connection, and will strive to restore church relations, if they have been severed, by urging attendance upon the services of the church and Sunday-school to which the family naturally belongs. He will seek the help of this church's minister in any plans he may make for furthering the family welfare, and, in this way, a spirit of coöperation between churches of different denominations will be encouraged.

I cannot leave this part of my subject without mentioning one other matter, though it is only indirectly connected with friendly visiting. The training of ministers in our theological seminaries should include a thorough course of instruction in charitable work. This would enable ministers to guide the work of their people in the best channels, and it would save them, moreover, from the discouragements of the conscientious worker who is striving to improve social conditions without any clear conception of the scope and limitations of such service. There are many clergymen whose experience and opportunities for study fit them for leadership in an attempt to establish systematic training in the seminaries. A demand from the laity for more experienced direction in church charity would also help to hasten the introduction of regular seminary courses in applied philanthropy.

CHAPTER XI

THE FRIENDLY VISITOR

I HAVE tried to make a number of specific suggestions in the foregoing pages, but it is needless to say that only a few of these are likely to be useful to any one visitor, and it would be fatal to apply them all to one family. In the effort to be specific, I fear that I may have been as exasperating as the cook-books, which, in a similar effort, will suggest, "take a salamander," or "take a slip of endive," when neither is obtainable. Cook-books have their modest uses, however, and the cooks who are most skilful in skipping recipes not intended for them will turn the others to the best account.

In avoiding the danger of representing friendly visiting as a pleasant diversion, I may have gone to the other extreme, and represented it rather as an arduous and exacting profession. It is so far from being this, that professional visiting can never be friendly. In fact, friendly visiting is not any of the things already described in this book. It is not wise measures of relief; it is not finding employment; it is not getting the children in school or training them for work; it is not improving sanitary arrangements and caring for the sick; it is not teaching cleanliness or economical cooking or buying; it is not enforcing habits of thrift or encouraging healthful recreations. It may be a few of these things, or all of them, but it is always something more. Friendly visiting means intimate and continuous knowledge of and sympathy with a poor family's joys, sorrows, opinions, feelings, and entire outlook upon life. The visitor that has this is unlikely to blunder either about relief or any detail; without it, he is almost certain, in any charitable relations with members of the family, to blunder seriously. Visitors have said to me that they could not see that they had been of any special service, though their friendly feeling for certain families made it impossible to stop visiting. These visitors who have no story to tell have often done the greatest good. "One of the women we had not seen since she first came to us some four years before," writes Miss Frances Smith, "and we remembered her distinctly as quite ordinary then. Imagine our surprise in finding that a certain dignity and earnestness, akin to that of the visitor, had crept into this woman's life, and found expression in her face and bearing. Such transfigurations cannot take place in a few weeks or months; they are of slow growth, but they are the best rewards of friendship." [1]

The rewards of friendly visiting and the best results of such work are obviously not dependent upon the suggestions of a handbook. As Miss Octavia Hill has said, success in this depends no more on rules than does that of a young lady who begins housekeeping. "Certain things she should indeed know; but whether she manages well or ill depends mainly upon what she is." Life, therefore, is the best school. Meddlesomeness,

[1] Proceedings of Twenty-second Conference of Charities, 1895, p. 88.

lack of tact, impatience for results, carelessness in keeping engagements and promises, will be as fatal here as anywhere.

When we are depressed by a family's troubles and are striving earnestly to find a way out, theirs seem quite unlike any other troubles. In a sense, it is true that they are unlike; but there are certain resemblances between human beings, even when a continent divides them; and, unsafe though it may be to administer charity by rule, it is more unsafe to administer it without reference to certain general principles. Many of the suggestions of this book are not of universal application, but, in bringing it to a close, I shall endeavor to state a few principles that apply quite universally to friendly visiting.

1. The friendly visitor should get well acquainted with all the members of the family without trying to force their confidence. A fault of beginners is that they are unwilling to wait for the natural development of trust and friendliness. "They expect to make a half dozen visits on a poor family inside of a month," says Miss Birtwell, "and see them

helped. Now, which one of us ever had our lives strongly influenced by a friendship of a month's standing? ... I once heard a sermon which made an impression on my mind that has remained with me for years. One of its main ideas was to get your influence before you used it. Many people seem to think that if they can visit a poor family, by virtue of their superior education and culture, they must immediately have a very strong influence. They do not get it that way. They must get it just as our friends get an influence over us, by long, patient contact, and by the slow, natural growth of friendship."[1]

Patience is difficult where we see so many things to be done, and it is particularly difficult where there is actual need; but the visitor does not go to act as a substitute for the forces, charitable or other, that have kept the family alive so far. He must confer with sources of relief that are or can be interested, but beyond this he must have the courage to

[1] Proceedings of International Congress of Charities, volume on "Organization of Charities," p. 21.

do nothing until he knows what is the right thing to do.

It is not possible to visit many families, but there are definite advantages in visiting more than one — the usual limit should be not less than two nor more than four. An advantage in visiting two families is that the visitor is less likely to be feverishly active during the earlier stages of acquaintance, and the contrasts and resemblances between the two give the visitor a better grasp of principles. Not only is a new visitor liable to err in overvisiting a family, but some families have too many charitable visitors. The New York visitor, who refused to go to a family on whom three charity workers had lately called, was wise. There are families so clearly overvisited that all who are charitably interested in them should be persuaded to let them alone for a while.

It ought to be unnecessary to add that the winter is not the only time for charitable work. Our poor friends need us quite as much in summer, though many charities are less active then. When we are away in summer we can write, and when we are in town for a short while we can often find time for a visit. Charitable work suffers from the tradition that the only time to be charitable is when it is cold.

Next to uninterrupted visiting as a means of getting acquainted, comes the power of taking our own interests with us when we visit. "In our contact with poor people we do not always give ourselves as generously as we might. Intent upon finding out about them, we forget that they might be interested to hear about us. Would it not be well if, instead of always giving sympathy, we sometimes asked it? It is often striking, if we tell them about the joys and sorrows of our friends, to note how they respond, often inquiring about them afterward. Such mutual relationship broadens their meagre lives, and makes our contact with them more human. A visitor, who has undertaken during the summer the families of another too far away to visit, wrote: 'I want to tell you what a matter of interest and pleasure it has been to me, in visiting your families, to find that what they really seemed to value was your personal friendship for them, and how they treasured any little incident you had told them of yourself and your travels.'"[1]

One who visits in this spirit always wins more of pleasure and of profit from the work. In fact, it is never the visited only that are benefited.

2. In getting acquainted, the visitor has the definite object of trying to improve the condition of the family. This is impossible unless he has a fairly accurate knowledge of the main facts of the family history. Charity workers often come to me for advice about individual families, and reveal in a few minutes' conversation that they have no knowledge of the condition of those they would help. The head of the family is sick, it may be, and they expect prompt advice as to the best way to help him; but they have not taken the trouble to see the dispensary doctor who attends him, or to find out in some other way the nature of his disease; or perhaps the boy is out of work, but they have not seen his

[1] Eleventh Report of Boston Associated Charities, p. 31.

former employer and know nothing of his earning capacity or references. Charitable skill is not a sort of benevolent magic; it is based on common sense, and must work in close contact with the facts of life. In other friendly relations we recognize this, and in our charity work too, whether by investigation of a trained agent or by our own inquiries, we must have the facts before we can find out the best way to help. One advantage of visiting under the guidance of a charity organization society is that a thorough investigation has been made of the family circumstances before the visitor is sent.

The following is a brief outline of the facts that should be known, if a plan is to be made for the family's benefit:

(a) *Social History.* — Names; ages; birthplaces; marriage; number of rooms occupied; education; children's school; names, addresses, and condition of relatives and friends; church; previous residences.

(b) *Physical History.* — Health of each member of the family; name of doctor; habits.

(c) *Work History.* — Occupations; names

and addresses of present and former employers; how long and at what seasons usually in work; how long out of work now; earning capacity of each worker.

(d) *Financial History.* — Rent ; landlord ; debts, including instalment purchases; beneficial societies ; trade-union ; life insurance; pawn tickets; has family ever saved and how much?; present savings; income; present means of subsistence other than wages; pensions; relief, sources, and amount; charities interested.

In addition to these detached facts, there is also needed whatever other facts will make a fairly complete brief biography of the heads of the family, including a knowledge of their hopes and plans. The statements of relatives and friends, their theory as to the best method of aiding, together with some definite promise as to what they themselves will do; the statements of pastor or Sunday-school teacher, of doctor, former employers, and former landlords; and the statements and experiences also of others charitably interested may be needed before an effective plan can be made.

Inquiries of present employers and landlords should be made with extreme care, if at all, as they might create prejudice against those we would help.

The outline here given of the facts needed is best filled in by a competent trained agent, rather than by the friendly visitor, whose relations with the family render searching inquiry difficult and often undesirable. But the mercifulness of a thorough investigation is that, once well done, it need not be repeated, and by saving endless blundering it also saves a family from much charitable meddling. Its seemingly inquisitorial features are justified by the fact that it is not made with any purpose of finding people out, but with the sole purpose of finding out how to help them.

3. Gathering facts about the poor without making any effort to use these facts for their good has been compared to harrowing the ground without sowing the seed. The facts should be made the basis of a well-considered plan. It may be necessary to modify our plans often, as circumstances change or new facts are discovered; but a plan of treatment

is as indispensable to the charity worker as to the physician. Our plans must not ignore the family resources for self-help. The best charity work develops these resources. If outside help is needed, it should be made conditional upon renewed efforts at work or in school, upon willingness to receive training, upon cleanliness, or upon some other development within the family that will aid in their uplifting. All this is suggested, not with a view to making the conditions of relief difficult, but with a view to using relief as a lever; or, as some one has put it, we should make our help a ladder rather than a crutch, and every sensible, reasonable condition is a round in the ladder.

Our plans for the benefit of one family must not ignore the possible effects of our action upon other families. This is a hard lesson to learn, but a plan that might be kind and effective, if there were only one poor family in the city, is often unfair and even cruel, because it rouses hopes in others which can never be fulfilled. In other words, we must be just as well as merciful. A knowledge of the neighborhood and of the circumstances of other poor families is necessary in judging of the justice of a plan, and here the criticism and advice of an experienced charity worker will be very helpful.

It is necessary also to guard against making our plans with reference to nothing but the present emergency. We must have a view to the future of the family, and must think not only of what will put them out of immediate need, but of what is most likely to make them permanently self-supporting, if this be possible. There are, of course, families that can never be made entirely self-supporting. These, if we consider only the cases for which it is thought best to provide outside of institutions, will be the exceptions; but in making plans for the welfare of such families we must try to organize help that shall be as regular and systematic as possible. Next to having to depend upon charitable resources at all, the most demoralizing thing is to be dependent upon uncertain and spasmodic charity.

4. In plans looking to the removal of the causes of distress, the greatest patience is

needed, and we must learn also, if we would succeed, to win the coöperation of others charitably interested. If our plan with regard to a family is likely to prove permanently helpful, and we are able to persuade others to work with us in carrying it out, we are not only helping the family, but we are educating others in common-sense methods. In persuading to an important step, the value of coöperation is illustrated by an instance taken from the Fourteenth Report of the Boston Associated Charities :[1] "A respectable woman, who had struggled for a year to keep her insane husband with her and the little girls, at great risk to them and the neighborhood, was persuaded in but a few days to let him go to the lunatic hospital. Of course, as strangers, our opinions were entitled to little weight; but by collecting the doctor's opinions and those of her own friends, all of which she had heard singly, she was sufficiently impressed to take the long necessary step."

5. Though we must make plans looking toward self-support, these are not the only plans

[1] p. 27.

THE FRIENDLY VISITOR 193

within the scope of friendly visiting. Some of the best visiting can be done after families are no longer in need. The entry "dismissed — self-sustaining" on charitable records has a very unsatisfactory sound to those who realize the further possibilities of friendly help. After a family has learned to live without charitable aid, there is a better chance of introducing its members to thrifty ways of spending and saving, to better recreations, and to healthier and more cleanly surroundings.

6. Our work as friendly visitors is an intensely personal work, and, unlike other charity, it is best done alone. We cannot visit in companies of two or three, nor can we talk very much about our poor friends, except to those charitably interested, without spoiling our relations with them. The district system of visiting among the poor, which is still the system of German towns and of English parishes, assigns a certain geographical boundary to each visitor. It has been called the "space system" in contrast to the "case system" of friendly visiting. The main objection to it is that it is not personal enough.

One who is a friend to a whole street is not felt by the members of any particular family to belong peculiarly to them, and there is danger, moreover, of more official relations and of small jealousies and neighborhood entanglements that are avoided by the friendly visiting plan.

The district visitor is the ancestor of the friendly visitor. Brewing a bit of broth for an aged cottager, reading beside some sick-bed, sewing a warm garment for Peggy or Nancy — it is thus that our ancestors lightly skimmed the surface of social conditions. It would ill become us to speak slightingly of the work of those who have handed down to us a precious freight of human sympathy and tenderness. If heavier burdens of responsibility, more serious problems and more strenuous ideals are now imposed upon us, we have also many advantages that were undreamed of a hundred years ago. Now, if we would be charitable, and possess any power of using the forces at our command, there are hundreds of avenues of usefulness open to us where formerly there was only one, and there are hundreds of agencies ready to help. We must know how to work with others, and we must know how to work with the forces that make for progress; friendly visiting, rightly understood, turns all these forces to account, working with the democratic spirit of the age to forward the advance of the plain and common people into a better and larger life.

Collateral Readings: "Friendly or Volunteer Visiting," Miss Zilpha D. Smith in Proceedings of Eleventh National Conference of Charities, pp. 69 *sq.* "Friendly Visiting," Mrs. Marian C. Putnam in Proceedings of Fourteenth National Conference of Charities, pp. 149 *sq.* "Class for the Study of Friendly Visiting," Mrs. S. E. Tenney in Proceedings of Nineteenth National Conference of Charities, pp. 455 *sq.* "The Education of the Friendly Visitor," Miss Z. D. Smith in Proceedings of Nineteenth National Conference of Charities, pp. 445 *sq.* "Friendly Visiting," Mrs. Roger Wolcott in Proceedings of International Congress of Charities, 1893, volume on "Organization of Charities," pp. 108 *sq.* Also Miss F. C. Prideaux in same volume, pp. 369 *sq.* and discussion, pp. 15 *sq.* "Continued Care of Families," Frances A. Smith in Proceedings of Twenty-second National Conference of Charities, pp. 87 *sq.* "Friendly Visiting as a Social Force," Charles F. Weller in Proceedings of Twenty-fourth National Conference of Charities, pp. 199 *sq.* "Company Manners," Florence Converse in "Atlantic," January, 1898. (This story is not a fair picture of associated charity methods, but points out one of the dangers of spasmodic visiting.)

APPENDIX

THE illustrations of friendly visiting in the preceding pages have been given with a view to elucidating some particular part of visiting work. Some of the following instances show the possibilities and discouragements of continuous visiting, and the last illustration emphasizes an important fact in the life of poor neighborhoods; namely, the unconscious but restraining and uplifting influence of good neighbors. On this same phase of the subject, see Charles Booth's "Life and Labor of the People," Vol. I, p. 159.

Home Libraries and the Visitor. — A visitor reports that "a library has been established in the room of Mrs. ——, where the boys of the tenement house meet every Saturday afternoon to receive or exchange their books, discuss with the visitor the books they have read, listen to stories as they are read or narrated, and to play games. This little gathering seems to have improved the moral and social atmosphere of the entire tenement house."

The woman who has charge of the library first became known to this same visitor over four years ago, when she was struggling upon the verge of starvation, and almost giving up in despair from the effort to support herself and her two children. Through the efforts of the visitor she is now comfortable and practically self-supporting. She has been made librarian for the tenement house by the visitor, and is proud of the distinction. The following are the exact words of the visitor: "She welcomes the children into her room, made scrupulously clean and attractive; and as she sits at her work and listens to their games and readings, in which she frequently participates, her depressed spirits rise, and she seems to gain courage, and to feel that there is after all something bright in her life." — Sixteenth Report of Cincinnati Associated Charities, p. 13.

After Five Years. — The C. family — father, mother, and eight children — were in a very depressed condition when I first made their acquaintance, five years ago. The father, who was a consumptive, had lost his position of travelling postman; the mother was ill; and the only source of income was a monthly pension of $8.00 and about $8.00 a week earned by the three eldest girls, who were saleswomen. The rent was $15.00 a month, and the family heavily in debt. I succeeded in finding them a house for $9.00 a month, and found assistance in flour, coal, and clothing. An unknown friend undertook to add $1.00 a month to

Mr. C.'s pension, and this paid the rent. Twice, when the girls were ill, the Golden Book Fund came to the rescue and made up the temporary deficiency. I tried to represent to them the dignity of keeping a roof over their heads by their own efforts. First, it became possible to dispense with the monthly gift of $1.00. Later, when the girls' wages were raised, Mrs. C. told me I need not provide fuel,— they would now try to do that themselves. One summer, whilst I was away, the youngest child died, and the funeral expenses were paid by the family, through much self-denial. Every year the girls have been sent to their friends in the country by the Fresh Air Fund of the Y.W.C.A., and once the younger children were sent to the Children's Country Home. The parents continued in wretched health; but as the girls' wages gradually increased, I was asked by Mrs. C. not to provide further aid, except in case of sickness. In 1891, Mr. C.'s pension was more than doubled, but they continued in their poor and unattractive neighborhood until every debt was paid, not forgetting the doctor. Last summer they moved into a larger house on a pleasant street, and have enough lodgers to pay more than half the rent. Mr. C.'s health has improved, and he has a light position at $25.00 a month and his meals. The oldest girl has married well, the two other girls are good workers, and my old friends are now well on their feet. During absence we have corresponded regularly. Mrs. C. has learned to come to me in every difficulty, and knows how gladly I share her encouragements. — " Charities Record," Baltimore, Vol. I, No. 1.

Persevering under Difficulties. — We are each year more strongly impressed with the importance and value of patient and careful visiting, even in the face of great discouragement, believing that sincere and judicious friendliness is invariably helpful, although it may be long before any apparent result is produced. Proofs of this are constantly coming to us, as in a German family which has been for the last six years under the care of one of our visitors. The family consists of father, mother, and five children, and, when first visited, they were found almost destitute, — the woman earning a little by picking berries in the summer and selling them, and the man by picking coal, — though they were well able to work. The visitor was received very ungraciously at first, and it was only after finding some work for the man, and showing a real interest in the children, that she gained any hold upon them. No really marked improvement took place until the children went to the Industrial School. Then the girls taught their mother how her work should be done, and it was with great pride that they showed the visitor how neat they had made their rooms. Work was obtained for the man as nightwatchman at $12.00 a week, and, after a while, he was able to pay off all his back debts. He is now always glad to see the visitor. Three of the girls are at work, and they seem a happy and prosperous family. — Tenth Report of Boston Associated Charities, p. 55.

Widow with Children. — A typical case of chronic dependence is that of a widow with six children. When she was referred to us, nearly four years ago, her children were very young, and she, though well-meaning, was stupid and inefficient. The problem was *not* whether aid should be given, — that was clearly necessary, for the woman could not earn anything with her little children to care for, — but if the aid could be given in such a way as to really benefit them. Relief was procured from the proper sources, — $20.00 a quarter from the "Shaw Fund for Mariners' Children," $2.00 a month in groceries from the city, and at times $1.00 a week from the St. Vincent de Paul Society. The visitor who first interested himself in the family, and who has been their friend and counsellor ever since, received the quarterly $20.00 for them, paid the rent with $13.00 of it, and gave the rest to the woman, who knew just what she had to depend upon, and learned to use it properly. As the children grew older, the boy went into a district telegraph office; and the girl, wishing to go into a store, asked the visitor to find her a place. He thought, however, that it was wiser to teach her how to find one, and, after suggesting some good establishments to which to apply, told her to get references from her school-teacher and others, and go herself to ask for work. This she did with some difficulty, and got a place; and when, after a time, she gave it up, she knew what to do, and had no difficulty in finding another. The boy refused to be apprenticed to a joiner, as the visitor wished, but is working hard in a place he found himself. The second boy goes to school, and sells papers. In summer, the visitor, with the consent of the Conference, has sent the younger children into the country to board for a month. He has taken pains to have the family live in a healthy tenement, and in many ways has insured their well-being. They are now partially self-supporting; and the older children are respectable and industrious, which we feel is greatly due to the influence that the visitor has exerted over them and their mother for four years. — Fourth Report of Boston Associated Charities, p. 40.

A Failure. — Gamma made his first application to the Charity Organization Society seven years ago, at a time when it was even more difficult than now to find volunteer visitors who were intelligent and faithful enough to make a careful study of the needs of families placed under their charge, or courageous enough to carry out any thorough plan of treatment in these families. The man was a German cobbler who had married an American domestic, and at that time there were three children, one of them an imbecile with destructive tendencies. The man said he was discouraged, that he got work with difficulty and had no tools with which to do it. Materials were furnished and members of the Society found work for him, but, this form of assistance not being very much to his mind, they soon lost sight of him, and it was not till several years later that the Society again encountered the family in a different part of the city, and a friendly visitor was secured to study their condition and try and improve it.

The visitor reported that the man was "discouraged," the house filthy beyond description, and that the life of the fourth child, then nine months old, was endangered by the imbecile boy, who was violent at times. Aid was given, and, the man's own theory being that he could do better in another neighborhood, the family was moved and otherwise aided by money secured from benevolent individuals. It soon became apparent that the man lacked energy. He was given to pious phrases, and was a good talker, but all efforts to inculcate industry or cleanliness were met both by man and wife with the excuse that the imbecile boy interfered with all their efforts.

At the family's own solicitation, the Society tried to find a home for the boy; after months of negotiations, he was placed in the School for Feeble-minded at Owing's Mills. This burden removed, the visitor redoubled her efforts to make the home a decent one for the remaining children, but without success. The beds were not made until they were to be slept in, the dishes not washed until they must be used again, and soiled clothing was allowed to stand in soak a week at a time in hot weather, until a heavy scum gathered on the top and the air was poisoned by the stench. The remaining children were unkempt and untrained, and the woman quite indifferent about their condition. The imbecile had improved at Owing's Mills, but, owing to a half-expressed wish of the mother's to see the boy, Gamma brought him home and refused to take him back again. The man's good intentions always seemed to evaporate in fine phrases. He was reported by the neighbors to be drinking, though not heavily, and one morning the visitor received a letter from him saying that she must take care of his family — he could stand it no longer and had left them.

One thing greatly handicapped the visitor at this time and later: the squalor of this family strongly appealed to chance charitable visitors, who helped them liberally because they looked miserable — helped them without knowledge and without plan. It used to be said that every American thinks he can make an after-dinner speech, and it might have been added that every American, or nearly every American, thinks he can administer his own charities judiciously. When we are mistaken in our speech-making ability, we ourselves are the sufferers, but the saddest thing about our charitable blunders is that not we but the poor people are the sufferers. The friendly visitor to the Gammas was a woman of unusual intelligence and devotion. Her failure may be traced to two causes: to the fact that she was not called in earlier, and to the willingness of many good church people to help quite indiscriminately for the asking. They went and looked at the home, saw that it was wretched indeed, and called this "an investigation." "Yes, I've helped the Gammas," they used to say. "I've investigated their condition myself." The way in which Gamma was in the habit of talking about the Bible as his best friend made a great impression on them.

The man's desertion of his family was a mere ruse. He was soon back again, and ready to profit by the help they had obtained. Moving from place to place to avoid rent, they were at last ejected, and the man, wife, and children, including the imbecile, found refuge in the stable of a kind-hearted man who took pity on them. The owner was alarmed, however, when he found the family making no effort to find other quarters, and fearing the imbecile might set fire to the place at any time, he applied to the Charity Organization Society to know what could be done. We offered the woman and children shelter at the Electric Sewing

Machine Rooms, until the boy could be sent back to Owing's Mills and the other children committed to the Henry Watson Children's Aid Society, and advised that the man saw wood at the Friendly Inn until he could get work. The man refused to go, but the woman and children came to the Electric Rooms, and with the coöperation of the Society for the Protection of Children, the imbecile was returned to Owing's Mills.

At this juncture the daily papers interfered with our plans for the children by publishing a sensational account of Gamma as a most industrious shoemaker, who had always supported his family until the hard times of the last year had thrown him out of work. Money was sent to the papers for the family. Gamma, who had consented to have two of the children placed in good country homes by the Henry Watson Aid Society, changed his mind, and the old story of indiscriminate charity and indiscriminate filth and neglect began all over again. The gentleman who had given them shelter thought they ought to have another trial. They had had six years' trial already, but this last one was of short duration. In four months their champion returned to say that the Charity Organization Society was right and he was wrong; that he had found Gamma drunken, lazy, and insolent; and that the children raised under his influence must become paupers and criminals. Again the family were ejected, and this time, before public sympathy could interfere, the two older children were committed to the Henry Watson Aid Society, and only the baby left with Mrs. Gamma.

Our advice to Mrs. Gamma was to return to her mother, who offered her a home. But the advice was not taken. Established in another part of Baltimore, Gamma renewed his attack on the clergy, and told one minister that he was a hardened criminal who had served a term in the Penitentiary, but, after hearing one of his sermons, he desired earnestly to reform. The latest news about the Gammas is a bit of information in which the charitable public will have to take an interest, however reluctantly, before very long, — there is a new baby. — "Charities Record," Baltimore, Vol. II, No. 8.

A Success. — The second family consisted of a respectable, middle-aged woman who had been twice married, four children of the first marriage, and the second husband. The eldest daughter had married, and with her husband occupied part of the house in which her mother lived. The other three children were young. The second husband was a drunken fellow, who did little for his wife's support and abused her badly. She had been to the hospital to have a serious operation performed ; and, although the operation had been successful, her health was still poor. When first known by the Conference the family were in great destitution. The husband brought home very little, the wife could not work, and one of the children earned a mere trifle. The rent was unpaid, and almost the only food the family had was oatmeal. The married daughter and her husband said the family had been long enough quartered on them, and refused to help them any more. The only work the woman thought she could do was sewing, and some of this was found for her. Diet Kitchen order was obtained for one of the children who was ill, and shoes were given to the others. Later, the Provident Association gave groceries. At this time the first visitor left the city, and a new one took charge of the family. She writes: "On first calling on Mrs. X., I found a tidy, respectable-looking woman, apparently in delicate health. Her face was almost that of a lady, and her manners were polite; but she did not make me very welcome. She spoke with affection of her former visitor, who, she said, had been very kind; but she presently remarked that she could not see why 'all these other people' had come prying into her affairs." On inquiry it was learned that after the former visitor had left town representatives of several charitable societies had called, and that one had hurt the woman's feelings by asking all kinds of questions without giving any explanation of his so doing. The visitor explained that she knew the former visitor, and had been asked to call in her place; and, after some sympathetic explanation, the woman seemed a little cheered. However, she resented the grocery orders she was receiving, saying that she did not wish charity — that she was willing to earn her living by sewing. "Why could she not have that instead of grocery orders?" As to sewing for the shops, she said she could not do that; for shop-work was too low paid, and she could not work on the machine. Plain hand-sewing was the only thing she could do. When told that certain sewing to which she referred was charity sewing, and was only given out in winter, she exclaimed, "Then it is not work at all, but charity, just like the grocery orders." When the visitor said good-by, she was invited to call again. She did so repeatedly, seeing the family once a week or oftener. On account of the drunken husband, some question was raised as to whether the groceries should be given regularly, but Mrs. X. stated that her husband never shared the food. He was away from home most of the time. Sometimes he would come home Saturday night and bring some money, and then he would take his meals at home; but, when the money was gone, he would go out for his meals, never asking how his wife and children fared in his absence. It did not appear that his disregard was due to his thinking that others would care for the family. The wife insisted that he did not think or care how they fared. He had sometimes left her for weeks, when she was ill in bed, and had never asked or known how she had been kept alive. He appeared to be so utterly irresponsible that he could not be made more so.

At the visitor's suggestion, it was soon decided that the younger daughter should take a place at service, where she could earn something and yet go home every night. Such a place the visitor found for her, and the girl was eager to save money to buy herself a coat for the following winter. The needs of the family, however, made it necessary to take the earnings for living expenses; but the visitor promised that somehow a coat for the winter should be forthcoming. When the employer closed her house in July, the visitor found a situation for the girl for the summer in one of the country towns. Of this time the visitor writes: "All the time I felt that the family were suffering more than was right. The children were fatherless and with a sick mother, and little A. was constantly ill, first one thing and then another, the doctors saying that he was under-nourished. Mrs. X. did jobs of washing and scrubbing as she could get them or was able, and the two children of thirteen both worked. So a benevolent person consented to take entire charge of the family, giving just what I should think proper. Accordingly, from that date to October 10 an average of $2.65 a week was given, besides $13.00 for clothes and other things. Also,

Mrs. X. and the two boys were sent to the country for one week. Notwithstanding this, Mrs. X. felt the summer a hard one. She was not a brisk or cheerful woman. She had suffered a great deal from the heat, and A. had diphtheria and other illnesses." In the fall it was arranged that the girl should again go to school; and the married sister finally offered, in order to make this possible, to board her and provide her with boots until Christmas. The Provident Association, after considering the case carefully, offered to give $2.00 a week and coal and clothing. The friend who had been giving all the help stood ready to give if more than this was needed. Two months later Mrs. X. had her husband arrested, and sent to the Island for a month.

In the winter Mrs. X. consulted her visitor as to the possibility of her giving up the Provident help and supporting herself by taking boarders. "She had friends all ready to come, and could arrange to hire additional rooms. All she needed was extra bedding. She felt confident of success. Her health was better than it had been for a long time, and she was improved in energy and courage. By dint of great persuasion, the Provident consented to give the bedding. They also promised to continue giving coal; but the other help, it was arranged, should stop. They had little hope, however, that the experiment would succeed. But the experiment did succeed, and better than I had anticipated. Mrs. X. proved a good manager. She made a comfortable home, clothed the children, and provided many little comforts of which they had long been deprived. She became cheerful and hopeful for the future. She seemed like a different person from the sick, discouraged woman I had known nine months before.

"When her husband came home from the Island, I feared he might disturb this prosperity, for he acted worse than ever; but in January he attacked her with a knife, so she had him again arrested, and sent to the Island for four months. She then told me she wished to take steps for a separation. I encouraged her in this decision, but was careful not to urge her, for I felt that such a step to be successful must be taken by her own desire.

"So, as spring approached, I hoped that better days had really come for this family. Unfortunately, however, in March a sad accident brought this prosperous state of things to a sudden end. On the morning of March 10, N. brought me word that his mother had fallen downstairs and broken her arm, and asked me to call as soon as possible. I found the poor woman in bed, with her right wrist broken, and her face and body badly bruised. She was in great pain, and so discouraged that it was pitiful. Her boarders had gone, and she found herself once more dependent on charity; but I felt I could say from a full heart that the help she now needed would not be grudged to her. For, surely, no one could help respecting her endeavor for self-support or could regard her effort as a failure; and, when her accident reduced her once more to dependence, her rent was paid for the rest of the month, she had a bag of flour and other groceries in the house, and $8.00 in money with which to pay the doctor for setting her wrist." The visitor adds: " I think that during this year's visiting Mrs. X. had really learned to regard me as a friend. At first I do not think she liked me very well, and I also found it hard cordially to like her. We were not naturally sympathetic. I am afraid that she often thought me hard; and she had a dreary, complaining way that tried me a great deal. But her good qualities commanded my respect and her misfortunes my pity; and on her my evident desire to befriend her gradually had its effect. Her first expression of real feeling was when she consulted me about her plan for taking boarders, and that was after nine months of constant visiting. She then said that I was the only friend that she had in the world; and later, when the plan was in successful operation, she told me that she attributed all her prosperity to me, and that she was a star in my crown. That she owed all her prosperity to me was of course an exaggeration. I could not have helped her had she not been the essentially decent woman she was. But, at the same time, it was true that, had she not been helped and encouraged when her destitution was so great, she would probably have lacked both the physical and moral strength, as well as the opportunity later, to stand upon her own feet. And, when her bad fortune again overtook her, it was much for her that she had a friendly visitor to turn to. She felt it so herself; and, as she lay moaning with pain, she sobbed out that I was the only comfort she had on earth."

After the breaking of her wrist, Mrs. X. was dependent for a long time, since the wrist did not knit properly, and her right hand was almost disabled. It did not seem as if she could ever get on her feet again. But after a time she wished to move to one of the country towns where she had acquaintances. The visitor went to the place herself to examine the chances, and decided that the plan was worth trying. The Provident Association gave $10.00 for moving and $10.00 more for a start. After that the visitor gave a little from time to time; but, for the most part, the family were self-supporting. The boy worked in a factory, the girl was employed by a neighbor, and the mother raised hens and vegetables. At last accounts the daughter was married. Her husband is of good character and prosperous. Both the brothers are earning good wages, the younger one having grown from a sickly child to a strong and hearty boy. The mother is successful with her poultry, and gets high prices for the eggs. The husband comes and goes as formerly, contributing nothing to the family income, but doing no special harm to any but himself. Certainly, the present condition of the family is a very happy contrast to that in which they were first found ; and certainly, also, these changed conditions are in no small degree due to the earnest and devoted efforts of the visitor. — Sixteenth Report of Boston Associated Charities, pp. 45 *sq.*

Unconscious Influence of Good Neighbors. — I would venture to say that there is not an immoral man or woman in neighborhoods known as disreputable, however completely he or she may have cast off self-restraint and regard for character, who has not daily examples of persons, close to such homes and haunts of vice, living honest and morally clean lives, and who is not, to a degree not consciously known, restrained and influenced by the contact. . . . Space will not permit many instances to be stated, but, as illustrating what I am wishful to make clear, I give two. In a court behind a street well known as bearing almost the worst character in Manchester lives a man, paralyzed, unable to leave an old sofa which has been his bed for months. He was in the Royal Infirmary, and there pronounced incurable, but likely to live years with ordinary care. He could have been taken to the workhouse hospital at Crumpsall, where he would have had careful nursing and suitable food. He has no dread of the workhouse hospital, and would gladly go if he had any hope of cure. He speaks most gratefully of his treatment at the Royal Infirmary. But there is no hope of cure, and his wife and he have determined to keep together while he lives, and he refuses the comforts of the hospital, and she refuses to let him go from her. She has made her home in this court, working in the room in which he lies, with only another room for their four children. She earns an average of 5*s*. weekly; her eldest boy earns at a situation 5*s*. more, and on what is left out of 10*s*., after paying 2*s*. 6*d*. rent, and buying coal and light, the six live. (The condition of things is now improved by the guardians deciding to take two of the children into Swinton Schools.) This is a simple and very ordinary story. But what is the effect of the woman's work? She says little to her neighbors. Her high purpose and her complete devotion to her husband and children have made other women ashamed of sin, and made men wish themselves worthy of women like her. She has no thought that she is doing anything but giving her life for her husband and children, has no knowledge of what the words " unconscious influence " mean — but none the less she is " a light shining in a dark place."

Another illustration. An old man, for forty years a laborer, never earning more than a weekly wage of

20s., who had brought up three sons (now decent working men, married, with families), became unable to work longer, and is allowed 5s. weekly by his last employer; the rent is paid by his sons, who also give an occasional shilling when they visit him. This is the whole income for himself and his wife. Some time ago when in the street he met a young woman whom he recognized as the daughter of a man who used to work with him. He saw that she was out for immoral purposes and spoke to her, telling her how sorry he was to find her leading such a life. As she appeared sorry and repentant, he took her home to his wife to take care of her until he could see her father. He found that the father had moved to Bury, having left his work in Manchester from shame at his daughter's disgrace. On the Sunday, when he could expect to find the father at home, the old man walked the seven miles to Bury and found his former mate, but could not prevail on him to take his daughter home. In fact, the father was very angry at being asked, and refused to listen. The old man walked back and told his wife that the girl must stay with them until the next Sunday, when he would try again. The next Sunday the old man walked to Bury and saw the father, who was somewhat softened, but still refused to see his daughter. A walk home again, and the old man and his wife settled that the girl should remain with them for another try to be made, and on the next Sunday he set out on the road, hopeful to succeed. The father this time gave way, and on the following Monday the daughter went home, and has since lived at home working regularly. The old man and his wife don't know that they have done anything "out of common," or anything more than ought to be done, "for a poor lass." — "Drink and Poverty," by Councillor Alexander M'Dougall, pp. 7 *sq*.

INDEX

Accident, damages for, 23, 104.
Addams, Miss Jane, 72.
Adequate relief, 157–159.
Adulteration of food supplies, 113.
Advertising, philanthropic, 148.
American Society for the Extension of University Teaching, 137.
Associated charities. See *Charity organization societies*.

Babies, care of, 77–78.
Bad temper as a cause of unemployment, 37.
Barnato, Barney, 10.
Barnett, Mrs. Samuel, 134–135.
Baths, cheap, 96.
Beale, Miss J. F., 130.
Beggars, 25–27; child, 88–89; and free soup, 149.
Beneficial and fraternal societies, 122–123; as a source of relief, 150.
Birtwell, Miss M. L., 182.
Boarding-out dependent children, 90.
Books, lending, 133.
Booth, Charles, 197.
Bosanquet, Mrs. Bernard, 18, 29, 48, 49.
Boston Symphony Orchestra, 135.
Breadwinner, the, as head of family, 17–19, 44–57; as citizen, 19–23; as employee, 28–41; intemperate habits of, 57–63; woman as, 72–74; child as, 81–83.
Brown, Miss Mary Willcox, 120.
Building and loan associations, 123.
Burial insurance, 110, 119–121.

Canterbury, Archbishop of, 172.
Catholic *versus* Protestant attitude toward the poor, 174.
Causes of poverty, 7–9; intemperance as a cause, 58; sickness, 95–96.
Character, 9.
Charitable agencies, multiplication of, 176–177.
Charity organization societies, 13, 31, 38, 55, 60, 62, 187, 189, 202.
Chattel mortgages, 115–118.
Child insurance, 122.
Child labor, 81–83, 111.
Children, of immoral parents, 49–51; of widows, 73–74, 158–159, 201–202; diet of small, 77; as breadwinners, 81–83; wayward and dull, 83–85; reading of, 86–87; training in citizenship, 87; begging, 88–89; protection from cruelty and immorality, 89–90; boarding-out, placing-out, and institutional care of, 90–91; cleanliness for, 99; sick, 101; insuring, 122; as an investment, 122; and stamp savings, 123; games for, 130–131; and relief, 146.

INDEX

Children's aid societies, 85-86.
Children's charities, 76-77.
Church, the, and municipal reform, 21; and relief, 160, 167-174; and poverty, 166-167; multiplying relations with, 168, 169; charities of, 170-178; competition in, 171-172; as a natural source of relief, 173-174; the chief source of the charitable impulse, 175-176; and secular agencies, 176-177.
Church workers, who ignore the breadwinner, 18; ignore neighborhood ties, 25, 27; ignore the fundamental conditions of family life, 44-45; ignore the claims of children to educational advantages, 81; allow children to be sent with begging messages, 88; prefer to administer spiritual consolation mixed with material relief, 144.
Citizenship, 19-23, 87.
City life *versus* country, 40, 82.
Cleanliness, household, 69-70; personal, 99.
Clergymen, difficulties of, in guiding church charities, 170-171; training of, for charitable work, 178.
Collection of small savings, 124.
Commodities, relief in, *versus* relief in cash, 161.
Common sense, charitable skill based upon, 187.
Compulsory education, 80.
Conditions, reasonable, in granting relief, 190.
Confinement cases, 48, 103.
Consumptives, change of climate for, 105-106.
Contagious diseases, 101.

Contentment not always a virtue, 127-128.
Convalescents, 104.
Coöperation, between churches and secular charities, 176-177; of the visitor with school-teachers, 79-80; with Sunday-school teachers, 87; with children's aid society, 85; with society for protection of children, 89-90; with board of health, 96-101; with dispensaries, 100-101; with hospitals, 101-103; with district nurses, and diet kitchens, 103; with educational agencies, 137; with relief agencies, 164, 201-202; with churches, 177-178; with charity organization society, 187-189; with others charitably interested in family, 192.
Correspondence with families, 184-185, 199.
Country life for families, 41, 82.
Credit, buying on, 113; better than relief, 149.

Damage and accident cases, 23, 104.
Dampness, 97, 102, 110.
Day nurseries, 77.
De Graffenreid, Clare, 25.
Deserted wives, 48, 73-74.
Deserters, chronic, 48, 205.
Dickens, 2.
Diet, 67; of small children, 77.
Diet kitchens, 103.
Dietaries, scientific, 66-67.
Discontent, social value of, 127-128.
Dispensaries, 100-101.
District nurses, 103.
District visiting, 193-194.
Doctoring, relief work compared to, 154-155.

INDEX

Dress and manners, taste in, 68.
Duplication of relief, 165.

Edgeworth, Miss, 2.
Education, 80-84, 92, 137-138.
Educational classes, 137.
Eliot, George, 2, 10, 34.
Eliot, Rev. Samuel A., 105.
Employees, 28-41.
Employer, as source of relief, 150; caution in making inquiries of, 189.
Employment, 28-41; fluctuating, 35; equalization of, 35-36; cautions in finding, 40-41, 201-202; facts needed in finding, 186-188.
Exceptional cases, 7.
Exercise, outdoor, 98-99, 132.
Experience, need of, in relief work, 163-164.

Facts, necessary in relief, 156-157; in treatment, 186-188.
Family, the, head of, 17-19, 44-57; essential elements of, 45-46; breaking up, 54-57; overvisiting, 184; brief biography of heads of, 188.
Family budgets, 125.
Financial history of family, facts in, 188.
Fluctuating work, 35.
Food, buying and preparing, 65-67; adulteration of, 113.
Forms of relief, 160-162.
Fraternal societies, 122-123; as a source of relief, 150.
Fresh air charities, 78-79.
Fresh air, prejudice against, 97-98.
Friendly visiting, and social service, 5; need of, 13; introduction to, 13; qualifications for, 14; and economic problems, 29; and employment, 36-41; men and women in, 41-43; and household economy, 65-69; and school-teachers, 79; and home libraries, 87; and the children, 91-93; and sanitation, 97-101; and sickness, 101-106; and thrift, 111; and savings, 124; and chattel mortgages, 116; and recreations, 129; and relief, 142-145, 183; and relief agencies, 164-165; and churches, 177-178; what it is not, 180; results of, 181; principles of, 182-195; patience in, 182-183; number of families in, 182; by correspondence, 184-185; mutual relations in, 185; and charity organization societies, 187-189; and others charitably interested, 192; best done alone, 193; distinguished from district visiting, 193-194; illustrations of continuous, 197-215.
Fuel, 68-69; saving for, 124.
Funerals, 119-121.

Games, 130-131.
Godkin, E. L., 21.
Gymnasiums, 132.

Health, 95-106; saving at expense of, 110.
Hill, Miss Octavia, 35, 128, 181.
Home, the, the unit of society, 44; relief should be given in, 145-146.
Home libraries, 86-87, 197-198.
Hospital care, 101; prejudice against, 101-103.
Howells, W. D., 70.
Humor, sense of, necessary in charity, 129.

Ignorance of English as a cause of unemployment, 39.
Imposture, 168–170.
Improvident poor, 112.
Inadequate relief, 157–159, 173.
Incapacity as a cause of unemployment, 34.
Incurables, 104–105.
Indiscriminate giving, 4, 6; by the poor, 25–27; weakens neighborhood ties, 27; weakens family ties, 45–47; to children, 88–89; materialism of, 141; results of, 157, 204–205.
Individual service, and social service, 5–6; dangers of, 7.
Industrial insurance, 120–121.
Influence, power of personal, 92–93; patience in gaining, 182–183; of good neighbors, 197, 215–218.
Instalment purchases, 24, 113–115.
Institutional care, 162; of children, 90–91; for chronic cases, 191.
Insurance, industrial, 120–121.
Intemperance, 7, 48–49, 54, 57–63; recreations as a cure of, 132–133.
Interference with individual rights, 12.
Interim relief, 154.
Invalids, chronic, 103–104; migration of, 105–106.
Investigation, 155–157, 186–189; caution concerning inquiries of landlords and employers, 189.

Jewett, Sarah Orne, 3.
Juvenile offenders, 85, 88–89.

Kelley, Mrs. Florence, 82.
Kindergartens, 79; first supported by churches, 175–176.
Krohn, Professor William O., 83.

Landlords who sub-let, 24; as creditors, 162; caution concerning inquiries of, 189.
Laws for protection of children, 91.
Lectures, free, 137.
Legal extortions, 23.
Libraries, free, 133.
Loan companies, 115–118; philanthropic, 117; building and, 123.
Loan exhibitions, 133–135.
Loans, 161.
Loch, C. S., 125.
Lowell, Mrs. Josephine Shaw, 54, 73, 118, 157–159.

Man of the family, often overlooked, 17; should apply for relief, 145.
Manual training, 92.
Married vagabonds, 47–57, 93, 146, 158, 164, 202–215.
Mason, Miss, 90.
Materialism of the charitable, 141, 171.
Medical service, cheap grade of, 100.
Men as friendly visitors, 41.
Migration of invalids, 105.
Money, relief in, 161.
Mothers' meetings, 74–75.
Municipal reform, 6, 21.
Music, 135–137.

Negro prejudice against hospitals, 102–103.
Neighborhood standard, and relief-giving, 163–164; and plans for permanent improvement, 191.
Neighbors, 24–25, 27; as a source of relief, 150; effects of relief upon, 163, 190; influence of good, 215–218.

INDEX

Newspaper appeals for individual cases of need, 147, 206.
Non-support laws, 53.
Novels, poverty in, 2; sociological, 3.

Odd jobs, 36.
Open spaces, 96.
Outdoor relief, public, 151–152.
Outings, 78–79, 131.
Over-visited families, 184.

Parasites, 11.
Partnership, with the poor in relief, 159; in plans for their welfare, 190.
Patent medicines, 100, 110.
Patronage, 10, 75.
Pauper burial, 118–119.
Pauperism not poverty, 11.
Pawning, 118.
Peabody, Professor F. G., 127.
Peabody, George, 135.
Pensions, for widows with children, 74; continued after need has ceased, 155; to supplement natural resources, 162.
Physical defects as a cause of unemployment, 38; as a cause of juvenile delinquency, 83–85.
Physical history of family, facts in, 187.
Pickton, Miss, 173.
Pictures, lending, 133-135.
Placing-out dependent children, 90.
Plans for relief, 154–157; changed with changing conditions, 155; based on facts, 155–156; for permanent improvement, 189–192.
Pleasures the measure of a man, 129.
Pledges, temperance, 61.

Policemen as distributors of relief, 19.
Political corruption, 21–23; and public relief, 151.
Poor, the, not a social class, 10–12; charity of, 25–27; treated as dependent animals, 125; partnership with, in plans of relief, 159–160.
Poverty, phases in our treatment of, 5; cure of, 29; problems of not so simple as they seem, 140.
Principles of relief-giving, 145–162.
Probation system for juvenile offenders, 85–86.
Protection of children from cruelty and immorality, 89–90; societies for, 89; laws for, 91.
Provident poor, 111.
Public distributions of relief, 147.
Publicity in charity, demoralization of, 146–148.
Putnam, Mrs. James, 76.

Quack doctors, 100.

Reading, 133; of children, 86–87.
Recreation, 127–139.
References, lack of, as a cause of unemployment, 37.
Relatives as a source of relief, 149–150.
Relief, policemen as distributors of, 19; of married vagabond's family, 50–54; of drunkard's family, 61; of children, 76–77; and hospital care, 102; of thriftless families, 112; and recreation, 138–139; a valuable tool, 140–141; friendly visitors as dispensers of, 142–145; six principles of, 145–162; with a future, 153–154; societies for, 153; in-

terim, 154; compared with doctoring, 154–155; with a plan, 155–157; adequate, 157–159; in work, 160; in kind, 161; duplication of, 165; church,167–174; as a gospel agency, 171–173; with conditions, 190.
Relief in work, 160.
Relief societies, 153.
Rent, 156, 162.
Richardson, 2.

Saloon, the, 57, 128, 133.
Sanitation, improved, 96.
Saving, 35, 111, 119–125; unthrifty forms of, 110–111; savings banks, 118–119, 123; beginnings of, 119; for burial, 119–121; for sickness, 122; stamp, 123–124; collections, 124; for fuel, 124.
School-teachers, 79–80.
Scott, 2.
Seasonal occupations, 36.
Self-help, resources for, 190.
Self-sustaining families, 193.
Sentimental charity, 4.
Settlements, 5, 8, 108.
Shaftesbury, Lord, 10.
Sham homes, 46.
Sick benefits, 122.
Sickness, as a cause of poverty, 95–96; outside hospitals, 103–104; facts needed in helping, 186–188.
Smith, Miss Frances, 181.
Smith, Miss Zilpha D., 36, 58, 79, 142.
Social classes, 10–12.
Social history of family, facts needed in, 187.
Social service, 5.
Soup kitchens, 148–149.
Sources of relief, natural, 149–150; relief societies, 150; public outdoor relief, 151; multiplication of, 152–153.
Spasmodic charity, 191.
Spencer, Mrs. Anna Garlin, 81.
Spending, 111, 112, 125.
Stamp savings, 123–124.
Strikes, 31–32.
Study, supplementary to experience, 15; of charity in theological seminaries, 178.
Suggestion, power of, 18, 71–72.
Suggestions about visiting not all applicable to one family, 179.
Summer visiting, 185.
Sunday-schools, multiplication of, 87–88, 168, 177.
Sympathy and sentimentality, 71.

Tact, 14.
Tammany Hall's charity, 20.
Tenements, unsanitary, 96.
Thanet, Octave, 3.
Theological seminaries, course of charitable instruction in, 178.
Thomas, Theodore, 135–137.
Thrift, 108–112; and wages, 109; includes spending, 110–111; divides the poor into three classes, 111–112.
Thriftless, the, 109–110, 156.
Trade-unions, 30, 32.
Training of charity workers, life the best school for the, 14, 145, 181–182; common sense in, 187; economic questions in, 29.

Undertakers and industrial insurance, 121.
Unemployed, in place of strikers, 31–32; number of, 33; treatment of, 34.
Unemployment, causes of, 33–40.
University extension, 137.
Unsanitary surroundings, 96–97; tenements, 96.

INDEX

Unthrifty forms of saving, 110-111.
Unworthy not a descriptive term as applied to the poor, 154.
Usury, 115-118.

Vagabonds, married, 47-57, 93, 146, 158, 164, 202-215.
Ventilation, 97-98.
Visiting, continuous, 182-185; illustrations of continuous, 197-215; patience in, 182-183, 200; illustrations of successful, 197-202, 207-215; in summer, 185. See also *Friendly visiting*.

Wants, social value of varied, 127.
Warner, A. G., 33, 95.
Wayward children, 83-86; girls, 216-218.
Widows with children, 73-74, 158-159, 201-202.
Window-gardening, 131-132.
Winter not the only season for charitable work, 184.
Wolcott, Mrs. Roger, 70.
Women as homemakers, 64-75; as breadwinners, 72-74.
Work history of family, facts needed in, 187-188.
Worthy and unworthy, 154.

PATTERSON SMITH REPRINT SERIES IN
CRIMINOLOGY, LAW ENFORCEMENT, AND SOCIAL PROBLEMS

1. Lewis: *The Development of American Prisons and Prison Customs, 1776-1845*
2. Carpenter: *Reformatory Prison Discipline*
3. Brace: *The Dangerous Classes of New York*
4. Dix: *Remarks on Prisons and Prison Discipline in the United States*
5. Bruce et al: *The Workings of the Indeterminate-Sentence Law and the Parole System in Illinois*
6. Wickersham Commission: *Complete Reports, Including the Mooney-Billings Report.* 14 Vols.
7. Livingston: *Complete Works on Criminal Jurisprudence.* 2 Vols.
8. Cleveland Foundation: *Criminal Justice in Cleveland*
9. Illinois Association for Criminal Justice: *The Illinois Crime Survey*
10. Missouri Association for Criminal Justice: *The Missouri Crime Survey*
11. Aschaffenburg: *Crime and Its Repression*
12. Garofalo: *Criminology*
13. Gross: *Criminal Psychology*
14. Lombroso: *Crime, Its Causes and Remedies*
15. Saleilles: *The Individualization of Punishment*
16. Tarde: *Penal Philosophy*
17. McKelvey: *American Prisons*
18. Sanders: *Negro Child Welfare in North Carolina*
19. Pike: *A History of Crime in England.* 2 Vols.
20. Herring: *Welfare Work in Mill Villages*
21. Barnes: *The Evolution of Penology in Pennsylvania*
22. Puckett: *Folk Beliefs of the Southern Negro*
23. Fernald et al: *A Study of Women Delinquents in New York State*
24. Wines: *The State of the Prisons and of Child-Saving Institutions*
25. Raper: *The Tragedy of Lynching*
26. Thomas: *The Unadjusted Girl*
27. Jorns: *The Quakers as Pioneers in Social Work*
28. Owings: *Women Police*
29. Woolston: *Prostitution in the United States*
30. Flexner: *Prostitution in Europe*
31. Kelso: *The History of Public Poor Relief in Massachusetts: 1820-1920*
32. Spivak: *Georgia Nigger*
33. Earle: *Curious Punishments of Bygone Days*
34. Bonger: *Race and Crime*
35. Fishman: *Crucibles of Crime*
36. Brearley: *Homicide in the United States*
37. Graper: *American Police Administration*
38. Hichborn: *"The System"*
39. Steiner & Brown: *The North Carolina Chain Gang*
40. Cherrington: *The Evolution of Prohibition in the United States of America*
41. Colquhoun: *A Treatise on the Commerce and Police of the River Thames*
42. Colquhoun: *A Treatise on the Police of the Metropolis*
43. Abrahamsen: *Crime and the Human Mind*
44. Schneider: *The History of Public Welfare in New York State: 1609-1866*
45. Schneider & Deutsch: *The History of Public Welfare in New York State: 1867-1940*
46. Crapsey: *The Nether Side of New York*
47. Young: *Social Treatment in Probation and Delinquency*
48. Quinn: *Gambling and Gambling Devices*
49. McCord & McCord: *Origins of Crime*
50. Worthington & Topping: *Specialized Courts Dealing with Sex Delinquency*

PATTERSON SMITH REPRINT SERIES IN
CRIMINOLOGY, LAW ENFORCEMENT, AND SOCIAL PROBLEMS

51. Asbury: *Sucker's Progress*
52. Kneeland: *Commercialized Prostitution in New York City*
53. Fosdick: *American Police Systems*
54. Fosdick: *European Police Systems*
55. Shay: *Judge Lynch: His First Hundred Years*
56. Barnes: *The Repression of Crime*
57. Cable: *The Silent South*
58. Kammerer: *The Unmarried Mother*
59. Doshay: *The Boy Sex Offender and His Later Career*
60. Spaulding: *An Experimental Study of Psychopathic Delinquent Women*
61. Brockway: *Fifty Years of Prison Service*
62. Lawes: *Man's Judgment of Death*
63. Healy & Healy: *Pathological Lying, Accusation, and Swindling*
64. Smith: *The State Police*
65. Adams: *Interracial Marriage in Hawaii*
66. Halpern: *A Decade of Probation*
67. Tappan: *Delinquent Girls in Court*
68. Alexander & Healy: *Roots of Crime*
69. Healy & Bronner: *Delinquents and Criminals*
70. Cutler: *Lynch-Law*
71. Gillin: *Taming the Criminal*
72. Osborne: *Within Prison Walls*
73. Ashton: *The History of Gambling in England*
74. Whitlock: *On the Enforcement of Law in Cities*
75. Goldberg: *Child Offenders*
76. Cressey: *The Taxi-Dance Hall*
77. Riis: *The Battle with the Slum*
78. Larson et al: *Lying and Its Detection*
79. Comstock: *Frauds Exposed*
80. Carpenter: *Our Convicts*. 2 Vols. in 1
81. Horn: *Invisible Empire: The Story of the Ku Klux Klan, 1866-1871*
82. Faris et al: *Intelligent Philanthropy*
83. Robinson: *History and Organization of Criminal Statistics in the United States*
84. Reckless: *Vice in Chicago*
85. Healy: *The Individual Delinquent*
86. Bogen: *Jewish Philanthropy*
87. Clinard: *The Black Market: A Study of White Collar Crime*
88. Healy: *Mental Conflicts and Misconduct*
89. Citizens' Police Committee: *Chicago Police Problems*
90. Clay: *The Prison Chaplain*
91. Peirce: *A Half Century with Juvenile Delinquents*
92. Richmond: *Friendly Visiting Among the Poor*
93. Brasol: *Elements of Crime*
94. Strong: *Public Welfare Administration in Canada*
95. Beard: *Juvenile Probation*
96. Steinmetz: *The Gaming Table*. 2 Vols.
97. Crawford: *Report on the Penitentiaries of the United States*
98. Kuhlman: *A Guide to Material on Crime and Criminal Justice*
99. Culver: *Bibliography of Crime and Criminal Justice: 1927-1931*
100. Culver: *Bibliography of Crime and Criminal Justice: 1932-1937*